Business Networking

FOR

DUMMIES®

A Wiley Brand

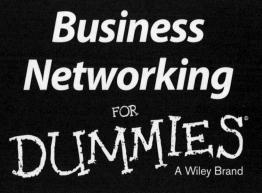

Business Networking
FOR DUMMIES
A Wiley Brand

by Stefan Thomas

Foreword by Brad Burton

FOR DUMMIES
A Wiley Brand

Business Networking For Dummies®

Published by
John Wiley & Sons, Ltd.
The Atrium
Southern Gate, Chichester
www.wiley.com

Contents at a Glance

Table of Contents

Foreword

. . . .

'Business Networking *doesn't* work!'

You're absolutely right . . . it doesn't, when you do it wrong.

You know what makes Stef Thomas an expert? He got it wrong, or at the very least witnessed someone else do it wrong; making mistakes in the field of business networking; as in, *all of them*. Every single faux pas you could possibly make, he's been/seen it all.

He got it wrong, as we all do when trying out new things. He's made those costly and often embarrassing mistakes . . . so you don't have to.

Back in 2008 when I first met him at a networking event, he was wet behind the ears, like many fledgling 'entrepreneurs' (also known as self-employed and very much skint). He had to juggle family, work, networking, budgets, confidence and self-doubt.

It hasn't always been easy for him, but with most things, often the difference between success and failure is *not quitting* even when it's tough. He's been close . . . but he has *never quit*.

Stef is a truly spectacular guy who behaves just like a normal one. That's what endears him to the audiences at his seminars and also makes him so amazing. He's unaware of his brilliance – whether speaking to an audience of a thousand or in this case, by writing several thousand words to support you, the reader, on your networking journey.

This is a modern-day book for a modern-day approach to modern-day networking. As you'll see, networking has evolved. It's moved on. It's no longer about vol-au-vents, chablis and sell, sell, sell.

Ironically, business networking is less about business but more about people. Stef recognises this, having spent the last few years deepening and widening his network.

Sometimes it isn't the best person for the job who wins it, but the one who's daft enough to keep going when others tell you you've got it wrong. In writing this book, Stef will likely stir up some of those critics who, over the years, have said his networking investment was wasted, to have networked his way from that first meeting, to writing this book.

Case in point: he's finally got his networking right.

This isn't just some puff piece. I've read this entire book from start to finish and so should you because, when you know what you're doing, business networking *does* work, and by following the blueprint that Stef has set down for you: *first you'll learn, then you'll earn.*

@BradBurton
Managing Director
4Networking Ltd

Introduction

*T*hank you.

If you're reading this little book, you've put a lot of faith in me. I appreciate that and have made every effort to pack as much as possible into this book so that you get massive value from it.

Thank you because this book justifies a lot of what I've blogged and spoken about at networking events for years.

Thank you because every person who makes a commitment to getting better at business networking makes the experience better and the opportunity greater; not just for themselves but for every other business person out there networking too.

Small businesses rule the world. Small businesses are the guys who supply big businesses, and provide extra employment opportunities. Small businesses also, of course, sometimes turn into big businesses.

The more that small businesses talk to each other, and exchange ideas and business, and acknowledge their vital role in the economy the better. Business networking is a huge part of that and can help to enable and facilitate that interaction.

I fell in love with business networking as an activity about six years ago because it offers so much more than most people realise. I've seen people's businesses and lives changed, including my own, through business networking.

I include a number of personal anecdotes in this book but the following is the one that nicely squares the circle of the story of this book.

After six years of business networking, I've attended over 650 networking meetings and posted on the 4Networking website around 18,000 times. I've attended the Business Startup Show and helped 4Networking (4N) on the stand every year for the last five years, becoming a Director of 4N in late 2012.

At a networking event after the Business Startup Show in May 2013, I turned to my neighbour and asked, 'So what do you do?' Sarah told me she was part of the team that creates *For Dummies* books, which I might have heard of, and I asked, 'Have you ever thought about doing one about business networking?'.

The fact is that I found the opportunity to write this book at a networking event. The fact that I put the hours in led to being sat next to Sarah that day. All the lessons that I learned from this great experience, I've squeezed into this little book.

About This Book

I've structured the book so that you don't have to start at the beginning; you can pick it up and only read up on the subject that you particularly want to find out about, using the index and table of contents.

I suggest, however, that if you have a few free evenings you do read it cover to cover. Doing so will not only massage my ego but also give you an overview and a broader knowledge of why business networking works in the way that it does.

Foolish Assumptions

In this book, I make some assumptions about you:

- You're new to business networking or have a desire to get better at it.
- You're involved in some sort of business or commercial exploit, whether you own the business or are an employee.
- You want to grow that business, sell more, develop personally and understand how to wring value out of your networking.
- You're prepared to read what I've got to say and work out how you can apply it to your situation, your business and your networking activity.

Icons Used in This Book

To help you navigate the content, all *For Dummies* books lay out key points of advice in an easy-to-use format. Look out for these icons throughout the book:

This icon points to useful takeaway ideas that you can immediately implement in your networking.

This icon highlights key information to bear in mind.

As you may have guessed, this icon is reserved for the bits of advice that you really, really need to take on board. Typically, in this book, it warns against what *not* to do.

This icon indicates a true-to-life example to help illustrate a point.

Beyond the Book

In addition to the material in the print or e-book you're reading right now, this product also comes with some access-anywhere extras on the web.

Find articles about networking around the world at www. dummies.com/cheatsheet/businessnetworking, plus an extra Part of Tens chapter at www.dummies.com/extras/ businessnetworking.

Where to Go from Here

Where do you want to go?

Do you want to get more out of open networking? In which case, go straight to Chapter 7. Do you want to join up your online and real-life networking? Jump straight in to Part III; you'll like it in there.

Alternatively, start reading from the next chapter and see where it takes you.

Part I

Getting Started with Business Networking

In this part . . .

- ✔ Know what to expect from business networking.
- ✔ Build your skillset, from public speaking to expanding your understanding of other businesses.
- ✔ Discover the many different business networking organisations and choose the right one for you.
- ✔ Read tips on networking at trade shows.

Chapter 1

Getting to Grips with Networking Basics

....

In This Chapter

▶ Deciding why to focus on business networking

▶ Examining where it all started

▶ Understanding what to expect

....

*I*n this first chapter, I explain why I fell in love with business networking, after a particularly shaky start. I also explain some of the options you have, and what you should expect if you're about to start networking.

Most importantly, I give you a few pointers and belie some of the common myths about networking, as well as plot a course from when the first person decided to go networking to where we are now.

Understanding Business Networking

I would love to be able to tell you where networking started and who it started with. It would be a brilliant start to this book if I were to give dates and historical evidence to support my contention that everyone everywhere needs to network in some way.

Focusing on business networking particularly, I reckon it started when a caveman (I'll call him Og, although the truth is I don't know) was really good at hunting oxen and his neighbour (who we shall call Ug) was well known locally for being able to make fire. Ug would always help Og make a fire and, in return, Og would give Ug some of his oxen meat; a sort of early barter arrangement.

Ug was one day helping another villager, Ig, to make a fire. Ig made spears and Ug mentioned, most likely by drawing on the wall of the cave, that his mate Og would be really interested in looking at Ig's spears and he would bring him along tomorrow to meet him.

Whether Og, Ug or Ig ever existed and whether there ever was an exchange of spears we shall never know. But I reckon that, when people first started specialising in something, that was when something akin to networking began happening.

Sadly, Og worked out that his best bet was to kill Ig, steal all his spears and keep the oxen meat. It always was a rough neighbourhood!

Tens of thousands of years later, a guy called Stefan walked into his first ever business networking event and therein started a love affair.

This affair began by attacking networking with brute force myself, simply by doing as much of it as I possibly could and forcing myself to find out how to do it better along the way.

But before I learned 'how?', I needed to understand 'why?'.

Starting with 'Why?'

You found out how to walk because you wanted to reach the exciting things that your parents had placed just out of your reach. The exciting things looked so good that the falls and the effort required to hoist yourself up, fall down and hoist yourself up again were worth it. After a few weeks of repeating these moves, you were able to take your first tentative steps. Then, you grabbed the first thing you could reach and put it in your mouth.

You learned to talk so that you could then give your parents feedback on the stuff they were leaving around for you to put in your mouth and ask them to put slightly tastier things within reach.

Around 17 years later, you wanted to travel further afield for more and tastier things, or wished to impress the opposite sex, so you found out how to use a complicated and expensive device (the car!) so that you could move around the country with relative ease.

At every stage, you first had a big reason 'why' you wanted to do something that involved lots of effort to learn how to do properly.

Had the 'why' not been there, had really tasty things been within easy reach, you may never have bothered with any of the above.

Noting the 'why' of networking

Today you have an opportunity to find out how to network, or how to network better.

Now I love networking. I love it enough that it's a huge part of what I do and these days I get an awful lot out of it. But getting it right may take a bit of effort and, like getting good at anything in life, you need to work out why you want to do it, so you can remember that if it ever feels hard.

What's your biggest challenge in business? What's the thing that keeps you awake at night or distracts you while you're trying to work? What would you like to be better at or have more of?

Write it down. Is what you've written down worth a bit of effort? If it is worth some effort, brilliant; if it isn't, then you're not thinking hard enough.

If you wrote down 'sharks', you're just being silly.

Whatever you wrote down (except sharks), you'll be able to solve that challenge or find that thing through business networking.

I reckon you wrote down something like:

- ✔ I've just started a business and don't know what to do next.
- ✔ We don't have enough clients.
- ✔ Our advertising isn't working.

> ✔ I don't know how to sell what I'm doing.
>
> ✔ I'm not confident enough.
>
> ✔ I need to start selling before I run out of cash.
>
> ✔ I've run out of cash.
>
> ✔ I need to know how to do something better.
>
> ✔ Nobody understands what I'm selling.
>
> ✔ There's too much competition for what I'm doing.

Do any of these resonate with you?

If you get good at business networking, by reading the rest of this book plus practising and refining as you go, you really can find whatever your business needs by building your network around you:

> ✔ More confidence
>
> ✔ More contacts
>
> ✔ More sales

Figuring out your 'why'

What is the thing that's going to make you really want to get good at this business and make it work?

Do you really want your business to work? Do you really want to get more out of business networking? Do you really want to answer another rhetorical question?

Go back a step further. Why are you really doing this? What is the thing that gets you up every morning and keeps you working on your business even when the going is tough?

Is it that you want to make a difference? Do you want your kids to have a better life than you did? Perhaps you want to take more holidays or to build up a decent pension?

I can't answer this question for you, but if you run a business, you're going to need to know why you're doing it. That's what gets you out of bed and working; that's what keeps you going when you have to put in the extra work and do the things you need to do, particularly as you're building your business.

Revealing my 'why'

Networking was well and truly outside of my comfort zone when I first started doing it – spectacularly so.

My 'why' was that I had to make my business work. I had no other way of paying the mortgage or bills. My 'why' was more desperation than anything else because at that point, in 2007, I was standing with my back to the cliff edge. I had nowhere else to go but forward.

I also realised at around that time that I wasn't a salesperson. I was great at a lot of things but I hated cold-calling and going door to door trying to talk to business owners (I tried it. Even in the summer it wasn't fun, so imagine doing it in the rain.)

I latched onto networking with a couple of big 'whys'. I needed to make my business work. And I wanted to do that without selling door to door.

Think about why you want this business to work. Write it down. Refer back to it if you ever question yourself.

Talking to Strangers (Ignore Your Parents' Advice)

One of the issues around networking is that it goes against everything you were told as a child.

I grew up in the 1970s (and will let you know when I stop growing up and become a grown up). Something that I was repeatedly told, by parents, teachers, nuns (Catholic school) and by the Public Information Films on the telly, was that I shouldn't talk to strangers.

Thirty odd years later, and I was walking into a room full of people who I didn't know – all of whom were strangers and all of whom I was expected to talk to!

This talking to strangers filled me with dread for a lot of reasons. Firstly, it went against those teachings from cleverer and bigger people than me when I was little. Secondly, I convinced myself that everyone else in the room was somehow 'better' than me.

I convinced myself that everyone else would have a better business, would be much more confident in what they were doing, probably have a better car and undoubtedly go on better holidays than me. Who was I, just starting out in the self-employed arena, to have anything in common with these giants of the local business world?

I learned a really valuable lesson in those early days, which I have had to learn and re-learn pretty much every day since. If I wanted to be any sort of success, I had to learn to get over myself and my little fears and insecurities. I had to push out of my comfort zone a little bit, then a little bit more, then a little bit more.

I was once told by someone not to think about going out of my comfort zone. Why would I want to do that? My comfort zone is comfortable. I like being comfortable. He taught me to think about going *into* my adventure zone. Instead of thinking that I'm leaving something comfortable, I now think about entering somewhere exciting. My comfort zone broadly involves me sitting at home eating crisps and watching repeats of *Open All Hours*. My adventure zone is akin to getting to go to Alton Towers every day and each time encountering a brand new and more thrilling ride.

No matter what your parents, teachers or kindly nuns taught you, ignore that for a while. If you're going to be any sort of success in business, you *will* need to talk to other people and a business networking environment, where everybody has chosen to be there and nobody has to worry too much about selling straight away, is the friendliest and most effective arena I've found for achieving that.

Knowing Who Uses Networking

People often ask me, 'So, who is going to be there?' or 'What types of businesses will be at the event?'

The truth is, all sorts of businesses use networking and all sorts of people go to networking events.

I've met the entire spectrum of business types and types of business people at networking events, from new start-ups through to owners of big businesses. No type of business is represented every time and not every type of business person is found at every event.

Try thinking about mining when you think about networking. Every type of business with every need and every purchasing requirement can be found here. Think of networking like this: you've established that there's gold here; you just don't know where the biggest nuggets are and where you'll simply dig without finding much.

But when you're mining, you keep digging and that's exactly what I recommend you do with your networking activity. Keep refining your approach by all means; keep finding better and more efficient tools to help you network. But keep digging.

What I sometimes see people do is dig for a while, then give up and go to dig another hole somewhere else, in a different networking group. Somehow they expect that, if they move from networking group to networking group often enough, they'll somehow stumble across a magical group of people waiting to buy from them.

Obviously, I'm a director of a networking organisation, so I have a preference. But find a networking organisation that suits you and stick with it. Find one where you're comfortable with the culture and the value that you can get from the network. Then apply every tool at your disposal to make it work.

Don't ever just focus on the people in the room; always keep in mind that you're also talking to everyone they know.

Think beyond the room. Every connection – every real connection – has value.

Remember, always, that whether your networking efforts work, or not, is ultimately your responsibility.

Rather than looking elsewhere for the 'right' people, have a look at your approach, refine, revisit, measure and make it work.

Thinking beyond the room

I first met Kathy in 2009 when she was a self-employed, sole trader, HR consultant. Kathy and I had a one-to-one and she became a client of mine. I was helping her write the content for her website, blog and email newsletters. Things were going well and Kathy's business was growing. After about six months, however, I got a call to say that Kathy was winding up the business. It turned out that she'd been head-hunted by a large retailer with over 3,500 employees in over 500 outlets. You see, before launching her own business, Kathy had held senior HR positions, up to director-level, at various well-known UK retailers. So I had lost a client, but a friend had got a great job.

About six months after that happened I got another call from Kathy, asking if I could, at short notice, do a presentation to the staff at their new store in Cardiff. Kathy knew that I could handle that, as she'd seen me present at various 4Networking events.

I did that presentation and, for the next year and a half, each month got three or four days' work from the same company. Kathy remained there as HR director for about four years.

The story moves on a little bit. Knowing that I had a large network of small businesses around me, Kathy used me as the 'go to' guy whenever she needed anything. She knew that I would always know someone who I trusted and had a good reputation as a supplier. My contacts saved her a lot of time and meant she didn't have to choose someone with whom she had no connection. In total, nine people from within my network received a referral to work with the organisation: a life coach, a health and safety specialist, a printer and a car leasing company, among others.

So my one-to-one had led to a very decent amount of work for me, plus referrals to other businesses too.

The story doesn't end there. One person had once turned Kathy down for a one-to-one. He didn't 'need' to talk to her when she was a 'little' business, but he got in touch with me as soon as he noticed that she was now with a big company, asking for an introduction.

Never underestimate the other people in the room and never judge your networking based on your perception of them. You never know who someone used to be, who they're connected to now or who they may go on to become in the future.

Realising It's Not All Funny Handshakes and Old Boys Clubs

One of my biggest worries when I first started going to networking events was that I had a stereotype in my head that I couldn't shake. I thought that the room would be full of people with much more business experience than me, all wearing very smart suits, and have the atmosphere of some of the uncomfortable business events I had attended early in my career.

Now, don't get me wrong. Networking events that *do* feel like 'old boys clubs' do exist, and they have a place. For example, you can find events that just welcome men, and events that only welcome women.

But for each of the above, you can also find at least as many networking events that welcome everyone, regardless of business type, business experience, dress code, gender or anything else. Plenty of networking events make everyone feel welcome and confident.

Some people are more comfortable with a strict structure, a defined dress code or only in the company of people of the same sex. But to my mind, every time you're at a networking event with a restriction, you're restricting the number of people you can meet, connect with and potentially do business with.

However, even in this section, I'm stating my opinion and my preference. What is important is that you choose a networking group or organisation that suits you and, throughout this book, I give advice and guidance to help you do so.

Finding Networking Opportunities

A networking opportunity to suit you really does exist, whatever your preference for types of events and format and whether you choose to look locally, regionally or nationally (or even internationally, come to that).

Chapter 4 of this book provides lots of guidance on finding networking opportunities but, in brief, start with recommendations from people you already know in business. If that fails, Google is your friend.

I will say something here, though. If you're starting your networking career, go to as many events as you can and work out what's the best fit for you. Think about:

- ✔ Where do you feel comfortable?
- ✔ What structure works for you?
- ✔ Are you being asked to commit to being there and, if so, is that a realistic commitment for you?

Try before you commit.

Following Networking Guidelines

Any networking group or organisation has certain guidelines, sometimes written and enforced, sometimes unwritten and simply expected.

I'm not a fan of rules anymore. I think that a lot of rules in business were created for a different age and many are no longer relevant. Who decided that people in business should dress in a particular way? And why does dressing a certain way make you more 'professional'? A suit is just a uniform.

One of the many extra benefits of networking is that you get to know other people's rules and decide whether you want to work with them or not. You may decide that it's in the interests of your business to follow some laid-down rules and guidelines, or instead that you went into business to make your own decisions and not follow other people's rules.

What networking can also give you is the confidence to decide such things for yourself. For a long time, I acted in the way I was expected to act and dressed in the way I was expected to dress, purely to suit other people's rules. Once I became confident enough to do things my way, I found that I was more relaxed and, as a direct result, people were more relaxed around me.

What I don't want to do in this chapter is make you worry, if you're about to embark on your first networking experience, that there'll be a load of rules that you have to abide by.

Turn up and be yourself and make sure that any networking event fits you before you commit to it.

Networking in a Nutshell: Different Formats

Networking involves lots of different formats and structures and I go into them in more detail in Chapter 6. Here, I just give you a flavour of what to expect, particularly if you're thinking of going along for the first time, or attending something different to your usual meeting.

Understanding unstructured networking meetings

You'll find networking meetings, and events listing networking as part of the format, which can best be described as 'unstructured'.

The best way to describe these meetings is that they're in a room full of people and you get to choose whether or not you go up and talk to the others.

Some people really thrive in these kind of meetings, and work the room with ease and panache, talking to everyone they have time for and always exchanging business cards. I deal with open networking like this in Chapter 7.

Bear in mind that if you're invited to an event or dinner that has something else as the main event but lists 'networking' as well, it probably means that there'll be lots of other people in the room. The networking probably doesn't have any structure.

Seeking out structured networking meetings

The type of networking meeting that I'm most familiar with (and personally prefer) is structured. These meetings are where the networking forms part of a proven structure or script.

I like this type of meeting because it forces me to network. In open networking situations, you may be tempted to simply chat to the people you know. In structured networking, the structure typically gives you the opportunity to talk to people you don't know as well.

Networking formats you're likely to encounter

I could write a whole book on the different formats of structured networking groups but will concentrate on the ones I know best and have come across most often.

Speed networking is often a person's first introduction to networking, as it's widely used at trade and business shows, not least because it creates a lot of energy and, undoubtedly, everyone gets to meet a large number of people. Put simply, at speed networking you get a minute to talk to someone, then you move on to the next person; you repeat this process until you've run out of people or the event has reached the end of its time. Speed networking is exhausting, frantic and lots of people enjoy it and collect *lots* of business cards.

Networking over a meal is really common and forms the basis of 4Networking, the organisation of which I'm a director. Typically, you meet with people over breakfast, lunch or dinner and a group leader, chapter director or chair runs the meeting to a script. This script always involves you introducing yourself to the group, as well as spaces for open networking and other parts of the meeting, such as a guest speaker and one-to-one meetings with other attendees. To my mind, the act of sitting and having a meal with others does help to quickly establish relationships and break down boundaries. There's something extremely social about doing that and the social element leads to a relaxed and efficient way of starting to do business.

Some local meetings have large numbers and you're split into tables where most of your actual networking is done with the other people on the same table as you.

If you're at that sort of meeting, get out of your comfort zone and sit with the people you don't know.

You can read more about this kind of meeting in Chapter 6.

Business networking and referral marketing – same difference?

As well as networking meetings using different structures, you'll also find that different organisations have subtly, but importantly, different aims.

You need to recognise that networking organisations structure themselves and their meetings differently, to ease the exchange of business between members, but in different ways.

Referral marketing is the process of attending networking meetings with the specific intent of generating referrals and leads from other members of the group. These referrals are typically passed on paper slips and generally involve the person giving you the referral having passed on your details to someone else who may need your service. These referrals are, of course, of different levels of value to the receiver. Some of them are simply the name of someone who may be interested, right through to a name and mobile number for someone who's interested, has had your service briefly introduced by the person referring you, and is now eagerly anticipating your call.

If someone's good enough to pass you a referral, please be good enough to follow it up promptly and feed back to the referrer how you got on. The easiest way to dissuade someone from passing you any more referrals is to forget or not bother to call the people who've been referred to you. A thank you is free, and goes an awfully long way in both business and life.

The purpose of your attendance and introduction at meetings with a referral marketing slant is to continue to educate the other members about your business, so that they know exactly what you do and who you'd like as a referral. BNI, the largest business networking organisation, has used this approach on a global level.

Business networking, on the other hand, is where you build relationships with the other people in the room, not just with the expectation of winning referrals from them. At business networking events and in business networking organisations, the relationships have value in and of themselves and can lead to business being passed, to joint ventures being formed, to trusted suppliers being found and to businesses being developed often far beyond what the business owner originally expected.

The purpose of your attendance and introduction at business networking meetings is to build and develop your crowd, those people who come to like, know and trust you and with whom you end up doing business or passing business to. 4Networking, I'm proud to say, has a massive network of joined-up business networking groups across the UK and in Australia.

Business networking and referral marketing require lots of the same skills, applied in slightly different ways.

Make referrals whether or not doing so is expected as part of your networking organisation. Be the person who gives. Be the person who others want to know because you're a natural giver. Give without expectation of return.

Take personal responsibility. If you're not getting any referrals, you need to work out why and do something about it. If you're not getting any business from networking, you need to work out why and do something about it. Never blame the other people in the room; they've got their own businesses and their own stuff going on. Refine and refine again until you make your networking efforts work.

You've already been networking without realising it!

Before you decide that networking isn't for you, please read this sidebar. Before you tell me that you're not the sort of person who goes networking, please read this sidebar. Before you decide to sit in your box room and aggressively wait for the phone to ring, please read this sidebar.

You're already networking and telling people about your business. You already have a brief introduction, which you tell people when asked what you do.

At the school gates, at the pub, at the golf club, at the swimming pool, at the gym, at your football or rugby club, at work if you're building your business on the side, on Facebook and wherever else, you talk to people.

You talk to people about what you do and you talk to people about what your partner does as well, so you already know how to introduce other people's businesses too.

You build networks within networks and circles within circles of people who like the same football club, the same rock band, the same reality TV programme. You form alliances with the other parents at pre-school and with the other people who go to the gym at the same time as you.

You know the other people at your church and what they do for a living. You know the other scout leaders and regularly go out for meals with them. You still keep in touch with all the people who were on the same adult education course as you in 2006 and, of course, you still keep in touch with your old school friends on Facebook and know what each of them, and their partner, does for a living.

You network already because that's what humans do. We're interested in what the other guy is up to and want to find out what so and so's husband actually does because 'in computers' doesn't cut it.

Business networking is nothing new, scary or complicated. Business networking is an extension and a refining of what you already do every single day.

Chapter 2

Exploring Different Aspects of Networking

*A*ll sorts of different people go networking and all sorts of people go networking for all sorts of reasons.

In this chapter, I look at networking for both the business owner and the happily employed. I also provide a few early thoughts on integrating networking into everything else you do, particularly your marketing and your social media.

What I hope is that, by the end of this chapter, you'll be set up with some ideas ready to set your expectations and business networking goals.

Networking for the Employed

Much of this book is aimed at business owners who want to use networking to build their business. I'm self-employed by accident and so have based a lot of this book on my own experience and the world as I see it around me.

But it surprises me that more gainfully employed people don't use networking to build their role and build their business. Certainly if I was back in a business development or account management role, I'd be all over networking for all sorts of reasons.

Networking has many benefits for anyone in an employed role, whatever that role is. Often the employee sees the benefits, but the bosses and the line managers only perceive that people are working if they can see them or know they're doing something that they understand and with immediately measurable results.

As the word spreads about networking as a mainstream business practice, more and more business owners want their people out there. Also, more and more business owners are using networking to grow their business in the early years and, once they take on staff, that activity becomes scalable.

Networking and co-working are going to become the norm as the definition of work changes in the near future. I can see that my sons' generation will see work as an activity rather than a place and a vibrant and ever-evolving networking system will become a vital part of what they do. I very much hope my sons learn some networking skills now that they can apply as they get closer to the time when they need to make a living.

The public sector is shrinking. Even the private sector isn't the safe haven it used to be. I was always told to get a job and stick with it; I'd be looked after and have a safe pension at the end of it. Does anyone really believe that's the case anymore?

I was quoted in Brad Burton's first book *Get Off Your Arse* as saying that 'being employed is just like being self-employed, but with only one client'. Sure, the sentiment is simplistic but, if I was employed right now, I'd be looking at every way to advance my career, secure my employment and make sure that I was the best at doing whatever I was doing. Networking has the potential to give you the ways and means to do all of that.

If you're employed and have stumbled across this book, or are wondering why networking is even relevant to you, please read on. Building, maintaining and evolving a network around you isn't just important to you in the modern work environment, it's vital.

Building your skillset using networking

One of the things that my sons will learn, hopefully earlier in their life than I learned it, is that your education doesn't finish when you leave school.

Those GCSEs (I've got O levels, giving my age away a bit), A levels, NVQs and degrees that you've got the certificates to prove? That's just the start. That's what you need to find your way into your first employment. I thoroughly recommend to anyone still of school age, and have done so to my sons, that they stay in formal education as long as possible. The longer you're there, the longer you have to build up the theoretical knowledge without all the distractions that working life brings with it.

But your real education starts when you start work. Remember that first day at work when no matter how qualified you were, you had no idea what to do and everyone around you was better qualified? Remember when you changed companies and all the experience you had meant nothing in the first fortnight you were there?

Hopefully, in your working environment, you get the opportunity for constant professional development. Hopefully, your employer is forward-thinking enough to realise that to 'upskill' every member of staff means huge potential improvements in efficiency. On top of that, having everyone else skilled to do everyone else's job, at least to a basic level, provides huge advantages to any employer.

But where are you going to pick up a load of the skills that you need to do your job or the next one up the pay scale?

The potential for networking as a learning environment is often overlooked. There are people both running businesses and in senior positions within businesses at every networking event I've ever been to, and these people have a huge bank of experience and knowledge that they often share in the ten-minute speaker slot.

The list of skills that you can use networking to attain at least a basic knowledge of is huge, but the list at least starts with the following:

- ✔ **Social confidence.** Just being in the, at first, unnatural networking environment is going to give you so much more confidence at any event you have to attend outside of your normal office environment.

- ✔ **Public speaking and presentation skills.** Everyone needs better presentation skills. In the modern world, everyone in every organisation is part of both the sales and marketing departments whether they think they are or not. Being able to briefly summarise what the organisation does helps any member of staff when they're asked, 'So what does your firm do?'

- ✔ **Basic business understanding.** Sometimes if you're employed, the basic mechanics and working of a business haven't been explained to you and, unless you did the subjects at school, you may not have a basic understanding. Finding out from business owners about basic economics and business matters helps everyone to understand how the business works 'behind the curtain'.

- ✔ **Business and social etiquette.** Even the most laid-back networking environment, such as the ones I favour, has unwritten rules of business and social interactions. I didn't discover these rules early enough and, despite my natural politeness, was caught out in my early expeditions to business 'dos'.

- ✔ **Networking!** Networking itself is a skill, which is, I hope, why you've bought this book. Being out there, though, and living it, building circles of people around you, assembling your crowd, is so valuable. Any member of staff, in any organisation, with a wide circle of contacts in other businesses is going to be valuable to that organisation.

I'm sure that's just the start and that I'll get tweets telling me that I missed such and such a skill off the list.

Do I believe this? Do I really believe it? Well, at the organisation of which I'm a director, 4Networking, we make sure that every member of staff, no matter where they fit in the organisation, goes along regularly to our own networking events. That way, they quickly gain a proper understanding of what's happening out there in the business world and how other business people interact. I've taken all of my sons to networking events as I believe the skills they'll develop there (the eldest as a musician, the other two haven't decided yet) are vital to what they're doing.

Meeting people in the same industry to swap ideas

Back in the day, in late 1988 and into 1989, a load of the estate agents in Oxfordshire used to meet at the White Horse pub on the corner of London Road and Headley Way in Oxford every Friday night after work. This event was my first opportunity to meet other people in the same profession and just chat. There'd be banter, there'd be estate agents notable by their absence every week, but a hard core appeared every Friday who realised that, while healthy competition existed, there was also no harm in at least being acquainted.

The car park was full of spotlessly clean Escort XR2s and XR3is with alloy wheels. The lounge bar was full of Marks and Spencer suits and white socks. We were nothing if not stereotypical in those days!

Two huge benefits for me were seeing that other people in the same profession were humans too and picking up the odd snippet that I realised I could use myself.

One of the reasons that anyone in employment should network is that it puts them alongside other people in the same industry, profession or business in a friendly environment.

Learning from people in the same field as you can give you a huge advantage in any environment. Come to that, learning from people outside your industry is also vital. Any organisation has a tendency to be a bit inward looking or to navel gaze. I try to be mindful of this fact every single day.

In the estate agency world, I used to look at what other businesses were doing that was new or could be applied to my own work practice. I watched as my MD at the time applied a load of lessons from the car industry (particularly how cars were marketed as a lifestyle choice) and applied that to how we marketed houses.

Having a constant stream of stimulation and ideas has the potential to give anyone the edge in their business. Networking puts you in an environment where that stimulus and those ideas are flowing permanently.

Keeping up to date with trends in your industry

In the bar at the White Horse, it was possible to get an indication of whether what I was experiencing from my office was being replicated across the county. If we were slow and everyone else was busy, then we needed to wake up and do something. If we were busy and everyone else was quiet, then we had a reason to celebrate our recent hard work – probably with another Guinness.

Talking to people in the same industry can give you a better idea of business trends than just examining your own management information.

If people are talking of new technology in your sector, you can get an idea, at the very least, as to whether others are implementing it. If a change in legislation is brewing relating to your industry, you get to find out not just the 'textbook' answers, but how it's affecting other people and what they're doing about it.

Talking to people in other sectors, as well, can give you vital business knowledge that you can learn from or can help in your understanding of something that's happening in your sector.

Meeting your next boss – career building and future proofing

Now, here's the rub. What if your next opportunity is right in front of you at a networking meeting, you just haven't spotted it yet.

Well, during my time networking I've seen people climb the career ladder as well as change career completely to do something they now really love.

On the other side of the coin, I've seen people find their best employee at a networking meeting too, someone with skills and an attitude that's just perfect for their organisation.

The above is why, if you're employed, you should make the effort to at least keep in touch with other people in the same industry, even if you're feeling completely satisfied where you are. Sometimes things happen outside of everyone's control, and being a step ahead of the competition when it comes to applying for a new job is always the right position to be in.

Do you know how to put yourself in the sights of any potential new employer? Well, you stay utterly committed and working hard where you are. But keep those other relationships going on LinkedIn and in real life.

Networking, for an employee, requires many of the same skills as networking for a business owner or self-employed person. Keep reading this book to discover many skills that you can apply everywhere.

Networking for the Business Owner

In this section, I'm back in my comfort zone – exploring the different aspects of networking for someone self-employed or building a business. Some of the aspects and advantages are obvious; some of them may be less so.

Networking still isn't the norm for small businesses. Those who make the effort reap the rewards; so please, if you're not already doing so, choose to be one of the few who do make the effort. You'll be in the minority and you'll have a competitive advantage.

Promoting your business

Most people come along to networking events primarily to promote their business and this reason is still the most obvious and prominent benefit.

Some networking organisations even promote themselves based on the amount of business their members are supposedly likely to win as a result of being a member; although that, of course, is based on many more variables than just turning up regularly.

Experts say that since the advent of Web 2.0 and social media no distinction exists between B2B (business to business) and B2C (business to consumer) interactions. All business is now P2P (person to person) because we're all connected through social media.

And I agree, which is why face-to-face, pressing the flesh networking is so important.

Promoting yourself by building longstanding and trusted relationships with other business people and employees of businesses around you immediately gives you a competitive advantage. Actually having a real-life relationship with you, and having got over the 'breaking the ice' bit, means that they find it much easier to start to do business with you.

Regularly attending business networking events means that you've constantly got a lot of real-life, warm relationships with people who know who you are, and know what your business does.

A few times throughout this book, I use the expression 'regularly attending'. By regular, I don't mean once a year. I mean regularly enough so that you're in almost constant contact with people. Attending a networking event at least once a week is sensible. Maintaining those relationships in-between is also sensible, but you can't beat being there in real life.

This attendance isn't instead of any other promotional work, but as well as and complementary to it. You can give real satisfaction when you meet someone at a networking event and they've received marketing material from you recently and can join up the marketing and the person.

Even better than that is when someone meets you first and then receives some of your marketing material and makes a special point to read it because they know you.

If you run your own business, if you're an entrepreneur or passionately self-employed, you need to be the biggest advocate for what you do. Networking can build you a crowd of contacts who will be passionate on your behalf – but that has to flow from you.

Be proud of your business and get yourself out there networking, applying some of the principles later in this book to ensure that your business is promoted in the best way.

Finding trusted suppliers: Real-life Google

Talking about longstanding and trusted relationships, your business, whatever it is, needs to rely on suppliers.

At the very least, you have someone who designs your website. You may have IT equipment that needs maintenance and occasional emergency support. You may rely on material being regularly printed. You've definitely got a mobile phone and probably a landline and broadband that someone, somewhere, has provided you with.

The links that lead to your business can be just as vital as what you do in your business itself. A lot of these things are like air; you don't really worry about them until they're not there.

Have you ever had your broadband go down? Has your main 'work' laptop suddenly and inexplicably refused to play ball? Then you know how disruptive these situations can be.

Where do you choose your suppliers from and on what basis do you choose them?

I'll tell you how it works for me. Over a period of time, some years in fact, I've built up a database of people I trust implicitly. I've based that trust both on my personal relationship with the people concerned and on observing how they've worked with other people.

Networking gives everyone the opportunity to find trusted suppliers. You get the chance to meet your suppliers and work out whether you can work with them or not, before you ever have to talk to them about business.

In the real world, you have a need, you Google it, phone the first couple on the list and then, hopefully, they're sat in their office and you're effectively interviewing them for the work.

In the networking world, you have a need, and you know a couple of people from your networking circles who supply that and who you can pick up the phone to and have an honest chat. Even if you don't know the people, you know that one of your networking contacts who you trust had the same need recently, and you can phone them up and see who they used and how they got on.

This way of working transcends testimonials on websites (and nobody has ever posted anything other than the good ones anyway) and gives you real information on who's brilliant and who should be avoided.

One of the great things about networking is that good news travels fast and if someone really is brilliant at what they do, people are going to be talking about it.

Bad news travels even faster and if a supplier is to be avoided, you get to know about it at the speed of light.

Communities tend to support each other and the opportunity to get real-time real-life information about which suppliers are the best, is something that even the mighty Google couldn't manage.

Because of my massive network, I have a reputation as someone who knows everyone and can find anything in business for my clients. One of my clients called me, back in 2011, wanting 5,000 branded and personalised Easter eggs. Twenty minutes later, I had a quote for them from someone who I trusted implicitly and was very happy to recommend. My client had a decent supplier, I'd passed on another referral and everyone was confident that the end product was going to be right.

Whether you're a buyer or a referrer, knowing that the person you're buying from or referring to is going to be sat opposite you at a networking event next week can be a huge benefit. It leads to exceptionally honest and mutually beneficial relationships.

Keeping up to date with trends in business

The opportunity and necessity to keep up with what's happening in the business world is vitally important for small businesses.

Small businesses that were out networking were among the first to hear about social media and how it can be implemented. Small businesses who are out networking are often the first to hear about what's going on in their town or community.

Small businesses that are out networking are literally part of the local scene, whatever local looks like to them, and have the opportunity to be up to date on business trends, local trends and technology trends.

Creating your virtual team: The future of business

The opportunity to assemble the right crowd for any project is another huge benefit of networking.

You have people around you who you trust and, as your business expands, you may be able to bring some of that talent in as and when you need it.

You may, if you use networking in its extreme form (Extreme Networking, I like that) constantly have enough trusted people around you to be ready for any opportunity and to have concurrent projects on the go at any one time as well.

As I write, my website is being redeveloped. I had no hesitation in assembling the team to do it, knowing the 'right' graphic designer for me, the right online developer, the right copywriter (that'll be me then) and the right blogging expert.

I am, at any time, a member of several teams, both within my 'proper' job and for various projects linked to it. Finding the perfect members for that team is never a problem as I have a constant stream of people around me.

Some big companies are now using networking as a template to build virtual teams within their organisations and many countries are now seeing co-working developing as an (almost) mainstream work environment where teams are formed and disbanded depending on the project.

Networking as Marketing

Marketing helps you to create the conditions wherein people want to buy from you.

Networking certainly fits as part of your marketing activity and networking shortens a lot of the process of marketing too.

In traditional marketing efforts, you:

- ✔ Collect contact details for your prospects
- ✔ Send marketing literature
- ✔ Follow up with a phone call and (hopefully) arrange an introductory meeting

In networking, you sit opposite your prospect at breakfast and have an introductory chat.

So networking can bring you closer to your prospects, shorten the process and, handled correctly, give you a steady and regular flow of new prospects and referrals to new prospects.

But networking also has other marketing benefits that can help with your other marketing efforts.

Clarifying your marketing aims

Networking, both online and in real life, has the potential to put you straight in front of your potential clients and prospects. Those who use networking as part of their overall business strategy have the opportunity to discover from their potential customers what they want, and use their networking partly for market research purposes.

Actually talking to other business people, without trying to sell to them, enables you to clarify not only what a new product or service will look like but also how to package it and how to most appropriately market it.

 You can ask your networking contacts what they think of a new idea or project at an early stage, plus get an idea of what they need and what problem they're looking to solve. This discussion in itself can help you package something new, or even repackage your existing offering to fit.

Reaping the benefits of business networking

You must be there to reap the benefits of networking; dipping in and out every so often simply doesn't work. That said, some businesses try the following as an approach:

- ✔ Go to a networking event – don't sell anything – before deciding that it doesn't work.
- ✔ Come back a year later and repeat.

But what happens if one of the people you spoke to last week decides in two weeks' time that they liked the idea of what you were doing and fancy a chat with you? Are you going to rely on them having your phone number and following up? Or is it likely that they're trying to remember the name of 'that guy who was here a few weeks ago'?

In order to reap the benefits, you have to be there when the benefits are ready to be reaped!

Networking Meets Social Media

My son once asked me whether everything was in black and white when I was little. He was, in his own little way, trying to work out what the world looked like before he was born and, from what he'd seen on the telly, it was likely that I spent much of my time fighting dinosaurs outside the village's communal cave.

I may not be quite as old as my son was trying to make me out, or constantly makes me feel, but just have a think for a second about how different the world is now to just a few years ago.

My sons, the eldest of whom was born in 1996, don't remember a time when mobile phones weren't the norm; in fact, they struggle to remember plain old mobile phones as they and their friends all have smart phones.

They think of email as old-fashioned and don't use it, favouring instant messaging and Facebook and Skype messaging instead. They're the generation who grew up with Facebook and used it to keep in touch with all of their friends when they weren't at school, particularly in the winter months when they were inside more.

Come to that, and to make me feel old, they don't even remember video tapes. I remember the first time I saw a video-recorder (my cousins had one) with a remote control; it felt like science fiction. My sons even think that DVDs are a bit old-fashioned.

Seeing the relevance

Why is any of the previous section relevant? Because when I started going networking, there was realistically no simple way of keeping in contact with the other people in the room in-between meetings.

I joined Twitter in July 2008, and Twitter, LinkedIn, Facebook and all of the others have completely changed the face of networking.

Now, in-between real-life meetings, I can continue to network and pass referrals to people without waiting for the meetings to come round. I can continue to strengthen the relationships online while continuing my regular real-life networking activity.

Making the most of social media

People often ask whether social media and online networking will replace real-life networking. People have even set up 'virtual' networking communities, with the networking meetings held virtually on Google Hangouts.

But, and I don't mean this in a creepy way, people like to touch other people. You'll find it difficult to develop trust online. People still need to press the flesh and look each other in the eye.

Perhaps you're thinking, 'But I don't need to meet the guy who owns Amazon in order to buy from the company. I never met Martha Lane Fox but booked a load of holidays through lastminute.com.'

But you're not selling commodities. You're probably selling a service. And even if you're selling stuff, or holidays, you've chosen the route of not being Amazon or lastminute.

Making the most of social media means joining it up with your real-life networking. Making the most of social media means using it as well as and complementary to your real-life networking and not instead of.

Real-life networking is powerful and vital for any business. Social media is powerful and vital for any business. Joining them up is exceptionally powerful. You have relationships from real life that you continue into the virtual world and relationships from social media that you continue into the real world.

Networking for the shy

I used to think that, as a naturally shy person, networking wasn't for me. But I've since realised, and it took me far too long to do so, that networking is perfect for the shy.

Being in business means that you've no choice other than to talk to other people. No matter how shy you are, if you want to make a success of your business you have to be out there and talking to people.

Networking places you within an environment and format that makes it easy for you to talk to people, with no pressure to sell or achieve anything at first. Sensible networking events even make sure that you're paired off with other people to speak to as part of the format, so you don't even have to approach people if you don't want to.

And those very acts, of getting used to talking to people and talking about your business, can greatly increase your self-confidence. I've watched people who consider themselves shy absolutely flourish using networking as a safe environment to develop themselves and their business.

If you're shy and need to talk to people about your business, you're going to have to swallow that shyness every time you pick up the phone to a new prospect or supplier. If you're out networking, you have to swallow the shyness the first time you go. The next time, and subsequent times you attend, you'll always come across people who you already know and like. Try it.

Chapter 3

Setting (Realistic) Expectations

....

In This Chapter

▶ Figuring out your networking expectations

▶ Matching your expectations to reality

▶ Cultivating relationships

....

A potential issue with networking is knowing what you should expect from it. In networking, possibly more than any other business activity, you have so many variables to account for that it makes a lot of sense to be realistic in your expectations, right from the beginning.

People's expectations of networking can be unrealistic, particularly in terms of the likely sales they'll make. Therefore, in this chapter, you think about what you should expect and, hopefully, be challenged a little to make sure that you're realistic about your expectations before you set off.

Recognising Why You Need to Set Expectations

Before you start any business activity, it makes sense to think through what the point of the activity is, which involves working out at the outset what you expect to get out of it.

Getting your expectations right helps in several ways:

✔ You feel more focused on why you're networking – vital on a cold December morning when you need the motivation to get out of bed an hour early and go to your networking event.

✔ You have a direction to work towards and understand what you're achieving.

✔ You're more likely to remain positive about the experience, whether or not you win business in the early days.

Only when you've decided what 'success' looks like can you make any measurement of whether you're achieving that success. In addition, setting your expectations early on helps you focus and gives you the motivation to persist with an activity (particularly if it takes you out of your comfort zone).

Put it like this: unless you've set your expectations, how do you know whether any activity is 'working'? Unless you know what you want to get out of it, how do you know when you're there?

Thinking about what You Expect to Get Out of Networking

Many people start off networking expecting that it will result in lots of quick and easy sales. They almost seem to believe – and perhaps networking organisations fuel this belief – that somewhere, magically, people are waiting eagerly to buy from them, and that this magical place is called networking.

If you start networking and your expectations are too high, you may be left feeling disappointed or with the belief that 'networking doesn't work'.

So before you network, ask yourself the following questions:

✔ What am I expecting?

✔ What do I expect results to look like?

✔ Have I set myself any expectations, goals or milestones that I'm going to work towards?

Networking is *not* a competition to see how many cards you can distribute, or how many cards you can collect. A card is not a connection. The only people who benefit from this approach are the people who print business cards (who are great people by the way). A connection is someone you've talked to and shown a genuine interest in.

At one of the very first networking events I ever went to, the organisers set a tongue-in-cheek competition. They challenged everyone to see who could collect the most business cards during the event. Even back then, I refused to participate and chatted to another kindred spirit while other people rushed around swapping cards.

Coping with your first networking event

Setting your expectations correctly for your first networking event helps you a great deal. If you go in expecting to come away with an order or two, you'll probably be disappointed.

If you're an employee, or have a business partner who isn't coming with you, then you may need to manage their expectations too. You're not going on a sales call here. The rules are different. Make sure that they're not expecting you to come back with signed orders and that they understand how networking works too. This way the people around you understand that networking is an important part of your working week and respect the time you spend doing it.

When you first start networking, people won't know you at all. You may have the best service in your sector in the world but understand the following: a small business owner is likely to be extremely protective of their business and their reputation and a large business employee has to justify any purchase to their bosses above them. People take time before they're willing to entrust you, or anyone else, with their business or refer you to their valuable business contacts.

So the first step in networking is to meet people. Your expectations of your first meetings should be nothing more than establishing a few contacts that are now warm, that you can now pick up the phone to and they'll take your call, because they've met you and shaken your hand.

My approach is to set no strategy at all for networking events and to approach each one with a completely open mind. I intend to just enjoy the event and, if I make some valuable contacts, then that's excellent.

If you're someone who does prefer to set a strategy, how about this list for a few things you may want to achieve during the meeting:

- ✔ Three people who you can reasonably now call contacts
- ✔ Maybe one loose agreement to follow up with someone after the event
- ✔ Successful delivery of your introduction
- ✔ One new thing that you learned from the speaker

After your first couple of meetings, you'll have met a few people; some of them you'll like and want to get to know better.

Expect the above to take time. Expect that before people trust you they'll want to jump through the various hoops involved in getting to know and like you first.

Knowing That Networking Isn't Without Effort

Marketing is often based on specific campaigns; networking, on the other hand, is a continuous process. This applies to both networking in real life and on social media too. Knowing that there's no end date for networking can be extremely helpful when setting your expectations.

Networking *is* working and the most successful networkers incorporate their networking into their working week. The people who benefit most from networking don't treat their networking as something they do when there isn't anything more important to do; they put networking into their diary just like any other meeting or activity and stick to it.

In this section, I offer you some basic time management advice that can help you get the most from each working day and ensure that you stick to your networking schedule.

Keeping track of your schedule

I was often told that you only have one set of 24 hours in every day. Find yourself a diary that suits you, paper or electronic, and use it to record every activity you need to complete, phone call you need to make, meeting you need to attend, social or family event you need to be at *and* every networking event or activity you're going to attend or undertake.

Personally, I use the Google diary, as I love the way it synchronises across every device I use. I'm a bit of a diary freak, so no matter which device I'm using I always have simple access to my diary and can easily book in new events and activities. I like the way I can colour code everything I do and give other people around me access to my diary so that my colleagues and family know where I am and what I'm doing so that they can check my diary before agreeing to anything on my behalf (although they regularly still do!).

I also love that the Rugby Six Nations website has a feature that puts every one of the matches into my diary at the push of a button every year. Little things matter so much!

Other people like Outlook or iCalendar; others prefer a paper diary or Filofax. You just need to find a system that works for you and stick to it.

When you put networking events, or indeed any meeting that involves you travelling somewhere, into your diary, make sure you include the travelling time to and from the meeting too. It sounds a stupidly obvious piece of advice but far too many people, when planning their diary, forget that instant travelling from one place to another still only exists on *Star Trek*. I look forward to *Teleporting For Dummies* sometime in the future.

Being patient

When you're into a rhythm and found the events and level of commitment that work for you, you must stick to it.

Not everything in networking has an immediate, or even obvious, payoff. The benefit you gain from getting yourself out there and building those relationships may take months or years to become evident.

You're not only building your relationships, strengthening existing relationships and continually adding new people to your network; you're also waiting for the opportunity to arise.

You see, as much as the other people around you may like and trust you, they may simply not need what you're selling right now. They may completely buy into what you're doing, but it may take time before they, or one of their contacts, has a real need for it.

The danger is that you may expend a lot of energy on networking, allowing people to get to know you and understand what you do and the benefits therein. And then you pull away, because it wasn't working quickly enough or other marketing avenues were producing quicker results.

People don't have short memories as such, but if you're not there, you're not constantly reminding people about what you do. You're not giving them those memory hooks, those little touches that mean that when they, or their contacts, need your service, you'll be at the forefront of their mind.

I wish I could tell you how much time is going to elapse before people start giving or referring business to you. Figure 3-1 shows that trust increases the more you get to know someone. I wish I could tell you exactly where the cross is going to be on the curve for your journey, at which point you hit that sweet spot where business starts to flow to you.

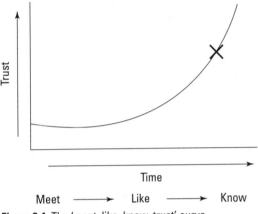

Figure 3-1: The 'meet, like, know, trust' curve.

But the variables are so huge; for example:

- ✔ How often people need your product or service (if you sell business cards, then most likely quite often; if you sell legal services, then maybe less so).
- ✔ How well you explain what you do.
- ✔ How you compare with other providers of the same product or service.

You're never going to know when people are going to have the need or desire for what you do. You aren't going to know in advance how much business they may ultimately put your way.

What I do know, and to an extent, what prompted me to want to write this book, is that far too many people give up their networking experience just at the point when they'd have gained the trust of others and started to win business and referrals.

If you're networking to further your career, exactly the same applies. The more trust you can build into the relationship, the more likely that someone thinks of calling you when they have a suitable position, or are looking for ways to bring you into their team.

Whenever I talk about these timescales, someone always says, 'But I don't need to build up trust in Mr Tesco or Mr Asda. I don't need to trust BP before I buy petrol from them. You don't see those guys wasting their time networking.'

If you have a product or service that people not only want but also need, and you have a delivery process to get that to the mass market, then you don't need networking. You don't need this whole process. But most of us do. If you're reading this book, I strongly suspect you either have products or services to sell and are looking for other business people or individuals to buy from you; or you're networking to take your career forward.

And, as it goes, many of the major banks, insurance companies and other large-scale service providers to small-business owners do engage in networking as it offers a fantastic way to show their brand off face to face.

Networking is all about relationships

You may have a new business to launch, or you may have an existing business and are about to launch a new service or product. You may be waiting for your new website to be ready or your new leaflets to be printed.

I find that people sometimes wait until everything's ready, until they've got all their ducks in a row before they start networking. But you're not conducting a marketing campaign, these are relationships.

Start now. Start meeting those people and building those relationships.

If you bumped into a friend at the school gates or were chatting to someone at the pub and they asked what you were up to, you'd tell them; you wouldn't say you had to wait until it was all ready. Treat your networking relationships the same as you do 'real life' relationships.

You don't do any harm going to networking events and talking about what you're launching, what you have coming up. You can still build the relationships and get to know the other people you meet at networking events.

If you really want to build your relationships quickly and build trust and respect with the other people you meet, go looking for opportunities for them.

Ask not what you might sell them, but what opportunities you might have for them.

Ask not what they might be able to do for you, but who you might introduce them to.

Just like in life, give before you expect to receive.

Chapter 4

Making Use of Networking Organisations

*T*he scope and sheer quantity of networking opportunities available to you if you wish to promote your business is huge; from simply meeting people down the pub, to events specifically for the purpose of promoting your business; from turning up and chatting to other attendees, to structured events with their own agenda. The networking environment has as many options as you can possibly imagine – and then some.

With such an overwhelming choice, you won't be surprised to discover that people often don't know where to start. Can you just pitch up, or do you need to wait to be invited? Is there an application process or is anyone allowed in? Do you need to be a particular type of business or based in a particular location to attend?

In this chapter we look at the various networking opportunities that exist, helping you to understand what opportunities are out there. We also explain the points of similarity in most events, and some of the specifics of some of the networking organisations.

Finding the Right Organisation for You

Different networking organisations and events do have their own culture and sometimes different events and organisations attract a different type of attendee. As well as recommending a 'try it and see' approach, this chapter also helps you to judge which is most likely to suit you and your style.

Before thinking about which is the right organisation for you, think about what you're looking for – particularly what type of business and what type of business person you want to mix with. You should step back and think about this for a number of reasons:

✔ Who are you hoping to meet at networking events? Prospects for your business? Business people who can potentially refer to you? Other business people you can learn from and share experiences with? Potential suppliers to your business?

✔ Are you looking for people who are based in the same geographical area as you? Or would you like to expand your business further than your town or county? Do you have aspirations to grow your business regionally, or nationally, or even internationally?

✔ Who are you comfortable with? 'Professional', suited and booted business people? More laid back and creative types? Tradespeople? Technical types?

✔ What sort of organisation or event are you looking for? Something with no structure where you just chat and hope to meet the right people? Something with a rigid structure and agenda to which the meeting runs?

✔ Are you comfortable with adhering to a set of rules and regulations within an organisation? Or do you consider yourself a free spirit who doesn't want to be tied down to someone else's rules?

✔ Do you want to pay for your networking or go to events that are 'free'? It sounds like you'd find an easy answer to that one but you don't.

✔ Are you considering attending regularly? Or are you thinking of dipping in and out?

So, there may appear to be a lot to consider, but one of the great things about networking is that you can try most of the options before you make a decision and, of course, you can change your mind when you've started.

Have a think about some of the questions above and write down some of your thoughts. Once you've done that, start looking at networking events and attend whichever events you can as a guest or visitor. You know what you're looking for and can start to judge if each event is 'right' for you to attend regularly or join as a member.

Start locally

Starting locally makes sense. Become familiar with how your local networking events work, even if in future you plan to spread your wings and take your networking activity further afield. This way you can at least build your networking confidence before getting out there.

Every town in the UK (and I'm sure in most countries) has networking events; both formal events for the purpose of networking, as well as other events where you find local business people congregating.

Towns, neighbourhoods, boroughs, districts and any other way you want to describe where you are tend to be quite supportive of their own. Getting stuck into local networking events gives you a good, safe, basis to build the rest of your networking activity on.

Match your business to the prospect

Before you think too hard about this, please think about how marketing works. When the big brands advertise on TV, is everyone who sees that advert an immediate prospect for their sofa? Or telephone service? Or toothpaste? Well, in the case of toothpaste probably yes but, for the other two products, the majority of people who see the ad won't be prospects *right now*.

I may be really happy with my sofa right now. My sofa is comfortable, reasonably new, I have claimed my territorial space on it in relation to the rest of my family and I won't change it for a few years.

Nevertheless, when I do come to change it, and thanks to the regular repetition of their television adverts, I know of two or three furniture retailers I'm likely to visit. I will try hard to get to them before their sale ends, of course.

Think about networking along the same lines. Don't get too tied up with trying to work out where your prospects are likely to hang out. You don't know who might not be your prospect today but may become your prospect tomorrow and you don't know who might know your best ever prospect.

By all means measure the efficacy of your networking as you go along but, at first, just get stuck in. I've heard stories of prospects for really niche businesses popping up in the most unlikely places. Equally, I've known people who spent so long trying to work out where the 'best' networking event was for them and their service that many opportunities floated by as they were waiting for the 'perfect' event.

Finding Independent Networking Clubs

So, let's start looking for networking events close to you. We start with independent groups.

Independent networking groups or events are typically organised by either local business people or a local chamber of commerce (see the next section). You're most likely to meet businesses who are based locally to the group and these events are fantastic for building up those local relationships. You're also likely to meet representatives of other networking organisations too.

Contacting your local chamber of commerce

Most towns in the UK have a chamber of commerce. Broadly speaking, the chamber exists to promote local trade and represent local traders both locally and nationally. For the benefit of this book, your local chamber is likely to run networking events.

You can find full details on the British Chambers of Commerce website at www.britishchambers.org.uk, which, helpfully, allows you to drill down to your county and find information about events happening in your town.

Finding local independent networking groups

As well as the local chamber, you'll probably find that your town has several independent networking groups. These groups are often set up purely altruistically by other local business people to ensure that local businesses are able to connect and network together.

Often, of course, the organisers themselves have raised their profile locally by organising the events, a *very* good reason to get involved in organising networking events yourself. But let's walk before we run.

- ✔ If you already know other local business people, ask them if they go to a networking event locally. Every single networking event anywhere welcomes visitors, so I'm sure that they'll be delighted to invite you along.

- ✔ Look through the local free press and in any local business publications. They're likely to have a list of events, including any networking events.

- ✔ Google 'business networking your town' or 'networking breakfast your town' or similar. Most events have their own website with information on who to contact to get an invitation.

- ✔ Have a look on LinkedIn at any groups relevant to your town or region. Often, networking events promote themselves through these pages.

You find just as many different formats and styles to the meetings as the number of local networking events. There really is no way to get to know them except for going along and experiencing them for yourself.

Joining Commercial Networking Organisations (in the UK)

As well as the various local and independent networking groups available to you, a number of commercial networking organisations also exist. These typically provide a regional or national network, which may or may not be joined up, and probably some other benefits as well.

Networking is itself a business. A number of organisations successfully provide networking opportunities to other businesses as their primary business, or sometimes alongside other activities such as training or providing services to business owners.

The following list isn't intended to be exhaustive but it does cover a lot of the major 'players' in the networking field, along with a basic description of their structure. In most cases the description has been supplied by the organisation itself; if it hasn't supplied anything, I've taken the description from its website.

So why should I pay when 'free' clubs are available?

The independent and 'free' networking events offer fantastic opportunities locally. So why would anyone even consider spending money on joining a networking group?

More importantly, if you want to take your networking seriously, why should you consider paying for membership of a group?

Consider your networking as a business investment. Whether you're looking at the marketing, education, business growth or any of the many benefits you get from networking, your activities in this area are an investment in your business.

Networking is also never completely free. Your time in your business is valuable. Your time is the one investment you can never get back when you've spent it, so any time you're going to spend networking is already costing your business – if you consider that there are many other things you can be doing with that time.

Added to that, you inevitably have the cost of travelling to and from each event, plus the cost of breakfasts, lunches and dinners to take into account.

So, from the outset, this isn't a free activity. Nor should it be.

Investing money in a networking organisation does a number of things:

- Firstly, if you have money in it, you're going to be committed to it. If you're treating your networking like you treat any other business expense or investment, you're much more likely to take it seriously. Think about this. If you've a networking event first thing in the morning and you've paid money to attend, you're much more likely to attend and plan the rest of your day around it. If you don't have to be there, you may well decide that you've more important things to do with your time – for example, those activities that *have* cost you money.

  Expand that to everyone in the group and it's likely that more people regularly attend as they're equally financially committed to being there.

- Secondly, if a large networking organisation is going to offer extra services and benefits, these things need to be paid for. Some of the larger organisations offer websites where members can promote their businesses or participate. They sometimes offer training or support services; or subsidised social events; or negotiated discounts on products and services. All of this requires administration and management by the organisation that needs paying for.

- Finally, you know that the other people in a paid networking group are treating their businesses seriously enough to want to invest in it too. If you're providing a product or service for other businesses, you've the confidence of knowing that the other people in the room have also paid. I have met many business owners who don't like to attend free networking events as they feel that, culturally, expecting anything to be free in business goes against basic business principles.

Many people gain huge benefits from the independent and free networking organisations and many people equally find that the more commercially structured organisations are a better fit for their business.

Go along and decide for yourself. Even the commercial networking organisations typically offer a number of visits as a guest or visitor before you have to make the commitment to join. Ask whoever invited you if you can try before you buy.

4Networking

4Networking (of which I'm a director), organises breakfast, lunch and evening networking events across England, Scotland and Wales, as well as a rapidly growing network in Australia.

Started in Somerset, England, in 2006 by entrepreneur Brad Burton, over 6,000 4Networking events are currently held each year, all of which follow the same format and style.

The 4Networking passport membership means that any member can attend any event anywhere. Many members take advantage of this and, rather than just attending one local group, expand their network locally, regionally and nationally.

The organisation has an iPhone and Android app as well as 4Networking's website, which shows where the meetings close to any location are.

In addition, 4Networking has an online forum at 4Networking.biz where all members can network with other members from across the network at any time.

The 4Networking meeting structure basically comprises open networking, followed by a meal during which each member and visitor gets 40 seconds to introduce their business. You get a speaker chosen from the members at each event and, uniquely to 4Networking, everyone has three 10-minute business meetings with other attendees in the room at every meeting.

You can find more details at www.4Networking.biz.

BNI

Business Networking International – BNI, claims to be the world's largest referral organisation and has chapters across the UK, which hold weekly breakfast meetings following a format designed to lead to referrals being passed between members.

Established in 1985 in the USA by Dr Ivan Misner, BNI sets up 'chapters' of professionals where only one person per profession attends the group, and they meet with the prime reason of looking for business opportunities for one another. BNI chapters operate under the principle of Givers Gain – by giving business opportunities to others, you should get business in return.

The BNI meeting structure is open networking, followed by breakfast and then a 60-second round for everyone to introduce their business. You then get a presentation by a member and the passing of referrals between members, which are made on paper referral slips.

BNI's website has further details at: www.BNI.co.uk.

Business Scene

Business Scene is clear that it isn't 'just' a networking organisation but it does hold successful 'Connections' events across the country.

Typically open networking events and held in the evenings, these events do bring together local businesses from across the networking sphere as well as people who don't network anywhere else.

These events also tend to have informative speakers on various business and networking subjects and are held in the evening, usually with an informal buffet and drinks.

Headed up by Warren Cass, you can find Business Scene events and details at www.business-scene.com.

FSB

The Federation of Small Businesses (FSB) is primarily a support and campaigning organisation, but it does organise networking events, made up of its members who are self-employed and small-business owners.

The events are organised regionally and have no set format, but if you're a member of the FSB remember to check with your local representative or on its website (www.fsb.org.uk) to see whether any networking events are held close to you.

NRG

NRG runs lunchtime networking events, primarily across the south and midlands of England.

Each event follows a light structure, with open networking, a lunch and 60-second introductions from each member, followed by a presentation from an expert speaker and finally a 'mastermind' session where members can raise business issues and concerns with other group members.

Dave Clarke runs NRG and you can find details at www.nrg-networks.com.

Women-only networking organisations

Several networking organisations only allow women as members or visitors – alas, this means that I don't have personal experience of them.

Two of the popular female-only networks are Athena (www.theathenanetwork.co.uk) and the Women in Business Network (www.wibn.co.uk).

Coming across Co-working

Co-working is networking in a different form. A global self-employment revolution is occurring, which many predict will see self-employment being the norm within seven to ten years in the developed world.

Work is no longer a place but an activity that can be done literally anywhere. However, the challenge has been that many have often, having no choice in the matter, worked from home. Home working is fine for some people as a way of life and is fine for others occasionally but for some it can lead to lack of motivation, isolation and being cut off from the buzz of the business world. Most businesses fail in the first year and the number one reason is isolation.

The other alternative until now has been the coffee shop. However, not only is that venue just as isolating but it's also noisy, gives you nowhere to charge your laptop and offers no security.

Co-working is now the third place, a real alternative to the isolation of home and the unproductiveness of the coffee shop.

Co-working hubs

Co-working spaces, or 'hubs' as they're commonly known, provide flexible physical workspace and often a range of support services, including access to funding and mentoring. The key thing that hubs offer is networking on tap – a community of like-minded people to connect, network and grow within.

Co-working is about community and, unlike hot-desking (where you literally just rent a desk by the hour or day), is about the network around you. Co-working provides a place to belong to and is a fundamental part of allowing you to collaborate with others. Within the community, you can find people who can complement and fill the gaps in your skills.

Co-working is the future of how many people will work and connect for business globally. For an example of a successful co-working hub in London, take a look at www.atworkhubs.co.uk.

 If you're just starting out, find yourself a co-working space to work from. Working at home in isolation can be a massive drain on your emotional resources. Having other people around you, even if just to pass the time with as you make coffee, helps you feel connected to the outside world.

KindredHQ

With highly formal networking at one end of the networking spectrum, KindredHQ's pop-up co-working events sit right at the other.

Founder Alex Butler says that KindredHQ events 'shouldn't feel like networking' but that inevitably the groups tend to 'gel', and collaboration and loose joint ventures form. Alex describes this as 'engineered serendipity', which I really wish I'd come up with as this phrase is such a lovely way to describe networking – even from someone who says that she hates the idea of networking.

At the time of writing, KindredHQ events are London-only, with no set format or timings. Further details are available at www.kindredhq.com.

Regus

Regus is very much a new player in the networking world but with a well-known and established name in the small-business arena.

Regus is launching Regus Connect in early 2014 with a stated aim of bringing together UK businesses, freelancers and interns to network and work under one roof. You can find more details at www.regusconnect.com.

Specialist and Niche Networking Organisations and Groups

In the spirit of collaboration, plenty of networking groups and organisations specific to one particular industry or profession are springing up, and many people use their industry's conferences and meetings as opportunities to network with other people in the same business.

Why would you want to network with people who, on the face of it, do the same as you?

Everyone develops their own speciality, or niche, or part of the job they particularly like doing. You can reap huge benefits from having people around you who fill in the gaps and can take on the work you don't do. For example:

- ✔ If you're a web designer, you may have loads of experience of Drupal, so wouldn't it be helpful to have someone with Wordpress experience in your contacts book?
- ✔ If you sell insurance and specialise in domestic insurance, wouldn't it be useful to have a relationship with someone who handles commercial insurance?

> ✔ If you sell houses – wouldn't it make loads of sense to have contacts who let houses?

Have a look at your trade press to see what events and opportunities exist for you to network with other people who do similar things to you.

Search LinkedIn to find groups relating to your profession or business. You can find loads of people and discussions within them that can be really valuable to you.

Networking with other people in the same industry can be hugely rewarding – if only to find out that everyone has the same challenges and problems as everyone else. The opportunity to moan with people who aren't in competition with you can be invaluable and give you renewed enthusiasm when you need it.

Understanding the Politics of Networking Groups

People can become passionate about 'their' networking group. Even though it makes sense to be a member of several (and have several interconnecting circles of contacts), time and cost often prompt people to join just one.

People who've bought something, so I'm told, often display 'confirmation bias'; that is, they look for reasons to support their belief that they made the right decision. Sometimes this includes ridiculing the perceived 'opposition' – that is, people who made a different buying decision.

A little like supporters of a particular football club (I don't follow football, which saves me all sorts of arguments and lots of time that I don't have to spend shouting at the television), people can become 'supporters' and sometimes avid supporters of their chosen networking group. Just occasionally, this evangelism can be off-putting to people new to networking.

If you're considering joining a networking organisation, visit several of them first. See what you think. Notice what you like and don't like. Find out whether the group has any special offers to encourage first-time members to join. And go with your gut instinct too.

You won't find a special group where a load of people are just waiting to buy from you. The same rules apply in networking as in commerce generally. No matter how good your product or service is, people buy when the time is right for them.

When you've joined, commit. Stick at it and resist the temptation to flit from one networking group to another, endlessly looking for the 'right' people who are waiting to buy from you. If people aren't 'getting' what it is you do, your approach is much more likely to be the problem than the make-up of the people in the room.

Running Your Own Networking Club

So why not do it yourself? You want to get to know other businesses; you're excited at the prospect of networking. Why not set up a networking group or club yourself?

You can gain huge benefits from doing so. You can become a local figurehead, you have a platform to present yourself and your business, plus there may be membership benefits from existing organisations or even the opportunity to network for free.

The opportunity presented by getting involved in running a group is generally massive, but as someone once said 'the trouble with opportunity is that it often comes disguised as hard work'.

Fortunately, many of the national networking organisations are constantly receptive to people who want to launch a group locally to them or get involved with an existing group. Some networking organisations even sell franchises to business people who want to run a group or several groups in an area.

You may decide, however, to go it alone and launch your own networking club or group rather than align yourself with a national brand. I've listed a few of the pros and cons of each in Table 4-1.

Table 4-1   **Going it Alone or Working with an Established Network**

	Pros	Cons
Going it alone	You decide the format, structure and timings.	You're starting from scratch and have to work everything out for yourself.
	You choose branding and get to write any literature yourself.	You have to negotiate with venues yourself.
	You invite who you want.	If there are upfront costs for marketing or websites, etc., you have to pay them.
	You assemble any team.	If it starts to go wrong, it's all on your shoulders.
	You become the figurehead and, if your network is successful, you can take all the credit.	
Getting involved with an established network	The format, structure and timings are ready-made and tested.	You have to stick to someone else's format.
	Marketing material is ready-made.	Costs are set by the national organisation.
	National marketing campaigns exist.	The culture and ethos of the organisation is set nationally.
	The organisation has an existing website or website template for you to use.	
	People can book into meetings using a booking system.	

(continued)

Table 4-1 (continued)

	Pros	Cons
	A support structure exists to help you make it work.	
	The organisation already has members who may attend your meetings.	

Remembering Why You Got Involved

Whether you choose to go it alone or work with an existing organisation, make sure that you're doing it for the right reasons. You're not failing in any way if you decide to be a member and never get involved on the teams, or go along to other people's networking groups and never run one for yourself.

If you choose to get involved, work out what you want out of it.

Never, ever, get involved in a network to help out someone else or the organisation. I'm inclined to be a generous person, particularly with my time, but a massive flaw exists in 'helping out'.

When you get busy, the first thing that goes is anything labelled 'helping out', as you're putting no value on it. When business isn't going well and you need to get stuck in, it's the 'helping out' that you sacrifice in order to make time.

Instead of helping out, choose why you want to be involved and commit to it.

When I first got involved in helping to run one networking group in Witney, Oxfordshire, I realised I could use my role to achieve several things, which turned out to be valuable to me and my business:

✔ **Enhanced profile.** I was known as the leader of a local networking group. So over and above any other attendee, I was one of the people on the team, the in- crowd, the cool kids. This gave me extra profile and visibility locally.

✔ **An excuse to call.** If I wanted to talk to another local business about my business, I could call and, instead of trying to sell to them, invite them to my networking group. This is a hugely overlooked part of the value from networking. Instead of saying 'Hi, I'm Stefan Thomas and I wondered if you'd be interested in talking about my marketing services', I could call and say 'Hi, I'm Stefan Thomas and I organise a group of local business people who meet every Wednesday. I've been asked to invite you along.' You'll find this a *much* easier call to make and you get the result you wanted – an opportunity to meet and chat to that business person.

✔ **Public speaking experience.** I was the group leader and it was therefore my job to deliver the script. Doing so terrified me at first but the group, of course, wanted me to succeed and this became somewhere to polish and hone my public speaking skills.

✔ **Management experience.** In an extremely safe environment I was able to lead a small team, in an endeavour that we all wanted to succeed. I used my role to pick up management and leadership skills and now put those same skills to use in a much 'bigger' environment where I have staff and team members all over the country.

✔ **A shop window.** As a small, work-from-home business, I missed the shop window that I had in my estate agency career. How does a small business make a big splash locally? My business was all about marketing and hype so I used my 'shop window' as group leader as my advertisement, showing off my skills. I promised that I could get lots of 'eyeballs' on any business, so I proved that by constantly getting lots of people to attend my networking group. I wanted people to see that I was efficient and organised, so I ran the group to schedule, with everything happening as it should. I wanted people to see I was energetic and threw myself at every challenge, so I ran the group with energy, creating a 'buzz' around the group as I went. At every step of the way, I made sure that what I was seen to be doing was matching up with what I said I could do.

When you take on a position in a networking group, you're on show whether you want to be or not. Just as you can use the enhanced profile as your shop window, people will be looking at you when you get it wrong too. Make sure that is the exception rather than the rule. If you're not confident in your skills or your determination to discover new skills, then consider whether a role like this one is really right for you.

Running a networking group on your own or with the support and assistance of a national organisation is a huge opportunity, but it does come disguised as hard work.

Using the platform; engaging the audience

Something to bear in mind is that no matter which networking organisation you're a member of, you're the one who has to make the most of the opportunities it presents. No matter how much support, training or help it provides, ultimately you're the one who has made the investment in joining and, like anything else you spend on yourself or your business, you're the one who needs to make the most of it.

Any networking organisation provides you with the platform – the networking meetings, website and any other opportunities it provides to promote your business to the other members and visitors – the members and visitors who are attracted to the organisation by its marketing.

If you find that you have household items to sell, you can advertise them by putting a postcard in your local post office or shop. But most likely these days, you'd put the items on eBay or Gumtree. Why? Well, you'd so because the audience is larger. These guys promote themselves and, as a result, more people look at your ad than if you placed it in the post office window.

No matter where you place it, though, you're still the one who needs to make the item and the advert as attractive as possible. You clean up the item for sale, ensure that all the relevant bits are there and dig out the original packaging. In order to put the advert together, you take the best photos you can; you take care to write the advert in a way that appeals to people reading it. You point out all the best features of the item itself and highlight them in the ad. You ensure that the price is worthwhile to you, while making the item attractive when compared to other similar items.

In short, the advertising websites provide the platform and the audience. You do the work to make sure that whatever you're advertising is as attractive as possible.

Business networking organisations provide you with the platform and audience. You make sure that your business is as attractive and visible as possible to the other members. You ensure that you put the effort in to become known and respected among the local audience.

Chapter 5

Networking at Trade Shows

....

In This Chapter

▶ Introducing trade and business shows

▶ Preparing for a show

▶ Working a trade or business show

....

*A*ll over the UK people are putting on various trade and business shows, general shows for business owners or specific shows for different professions, industries and trades.

While the main thrust of these events is typically trade stands wishing to sell to attendees, people can often be found networking as well. Sometimes the networking is explicit and advertised as such but, even if not, you can often find opportunities to network and make new contacts.

Knowing What to Expect from a Trade Show

Trade shows and business shows (the terms are pretty interchangeable; you may also find them described as 'expos') take place in pretty much every town and city in the UK. At the show itself are a number of trade stands or exhibits with products or services relevant to the audience at that show. Most shows have a programme of events including speakers, seminars, workshops and networking events.

The two types of people at business shows are:

- ✓ **The exhibitor** who has paid for a stand at the show to demonstrate their products or services.

- ✓ **The attendee** who comes to meet other people, have a look at the exhibitors' stands and learn from some of the speakers at the show.

Something well worth bearing in mind in the scope of this book is that a number of networking organisations themselves exhibit at trade and business shows; some even have taster sessions for their events. It may be a good opportunity to meet some of the local team so that when you first attend an event, you've already met a couple of people.

The Great British Business Show

The Great British Business Show incorporates what used to be the Business StartUp show and has been running since 2000.

Now running twice a year (once in the spring and once in the autumn) and alternating between London's Olympia and ExCeL venues, this show really is well worth a visit if you're a business owner or self-employed. You get to see how lots of small and medium businesses present themselves at shows, you can take part in several formal networking opportunities including speed networking and organised one to ones, plus you can attend seminars held by speakers on all sorts of subjects relating to small business.

If you choose to, you can pack a lot into your six or eight hours at the show, which, for that reason, attracts people from all over the UK. You can find more information at www.greatbritishbusinessshow.co.uk/.

The Welsh Business Shows

The Welsh Business Shows, which run annually in both Cardiff and Swansea, aim to bring together businesses from across Wales. The shows feature many exhibitors, from businesses of all sizes, as well as speakers, seminars and workshops.

Extremely welcoming and refreshingly relaxed, the shows always have many opportunities to network informally, as well as speed networking events.

More information on The Welsh Business Shows, including details of forthcoming events, can be found at www.the welshbusinessshow.co.uk/.

New Start Scotland

Running once a year in Glasgow, New Start Scotland – despite its name – features exhibitors and speakers from all over the UK. This trade show includes lots of information on starting a business and running a business plus a mixture of motivational and educational speakers.

The SECC venue is easy to get to and, if you're in Scotland or the north of England, this one is well worth getting to. Access the details at www.newstartscotland.com/.

Finding Local and National Trade Shows

You sometimes hear about local and national trade shows because they're advertised in the press, but that isn't always the case. Here are a few ways to ensure that you do find them and are kept up to date:

- ✔ **Keep an eye on your local business press.** Most counties have a business publication or, at the very least, business pages in the local or regional newspaper. Keep an eye on the ads to see whether an event is coming up near you.

- ✔ **Google it.** 'Business Show Milton Keynes' or 'Business Exhibition Oxfordshire' or something along those lines gives you a good start, using your preferred location. You may also bring up results for shows that have happened in the past so you can see whether the same organisation is running them again.

- ✔ **Search on LinkedIn for LinkedIn groups related to your town or county.** You may find a group for a specific exhibition or local groups that the exhibition may promote itself within.

✔ **Use the Twitter search tool to find Twitter accounts in your locality.** If you don't know how to achieve this feat already, go to https://twitter.com/search-advanced and use the 'Near This Place' field, where you can type in anything you like. Any business show worth attending has a Twitter account, which inevitably tweets forthcoming details.

✔ **Look out for your local hashtag hour on Twitter.** These are a relatively new use for Twitter but work something along these lines. Local business people tweet during a certain time on Twitter and using a particular hashtag. For example, if you search Twitter for #oxonhour, you see that every Wednesday evening between 8:00 p.m. and 9:00 p.m. Oxfordshire business owners tweet and add the #oxonhour hashtag to their tweets. Any business-related event locally is bound to be promoted here. This method is also a fab way to find other like-minded local businesses.

✔ **Look out for people promoting the events at local networking events.** Yes – networking events promote themselves at networking events!

Making Your Trade Show Experience a Success

Before you decide that you really should attend a business show and try to sell your stuff to all the exhibitors, just consider a couple of things for me.

Acting in this way is, at best, impolite and, at worst, possibly detrimental to the business of the person you're approaching.

The exhibitor has paid to be there. They've paid hundreds or thousands of pounds for their space. Plus, they've furnished the space, which has probably been expensive. Plus, they have people manning the stand, which costs, at the very least, a whole load of their time.

Their primary focus is going to be on introducing their stuff to attendees. Their time at the show is incredibly precious. So your approach is unlikely to be welcome as (a) they've invested in their business by paying for a stand and you've just pitched up, and (b) at a busy show, every second you're trying to sell to them they're missing the potential opportunities walking past. In addition, when that exhibitor leaves the show, at the end of a tiring couple of days for them, are they really going to remember you and your pitch? Of course not; they're much more focused on the leads they need to follow up and wanting to commit their time after the show to doing that.

Or they may just want to get home and have a glass of wine!

Networking at trade shows, big or small

The trade shows do present a major opportunity to network, however, and giving your approach some thought can really prove worthwhile.

Before attending any trade show or business show, ensure that you've plenty of business cards with you and something to make notes on (in case the people you meet don't have business cards with them).

Take a look through the list of seminars and workshops and register yourself for any that you like the sound of. You should be able to achieve a number of things here. Firstly, and hopefully, you can discover something from the seminar or workshop itself (in fact, you always will so make sure that you go intending to learn something, however small). Secondly, you now have something in common with everyone else in the room – you and they have all chosen to go to the same seminar.

So, at an opportune moment, turn to the person next to you and ask him what he thought. Did he get something from it? You've both decided that you had something to pick up from this seminar after all, so maybe your business and his business have other similarities? Ask him if he'd like to connect on LinkedIn or somewhere else on social media and exchange cards or contact details. If you've made notes on the event, offer to share them with him.

Someone who came to the same seminar as me at last year's Great British Business Show in London took a video of it. We got chatting afterwards and he offered to send me a link once he'd uploaded it. He and I are now regularly in contact, we are connected on LinkedIn and, when the opportunity arises, I'll have a coffee with him and find out more about his business. Funny thing is, I feel a little sense of obligation because he was kind enough to share his video with me.

Try to introduce yourself to the presenter or speaker at the end. Comment on what you enjoyed about the presentation. Ask whether he'd mind if you connected with him on LinkedIn or Twitter. Many presenters now give out their Twitter handle during their presentation. You then have the opportunity to give them feedback online too. No speaker I have ever met objects to attendees connecting with them afterwards. We find it quite flattering, to be honest.

Becoming part of the crowd

The simplest way to be seen at trade shows and business shows is to exhibit. Many shows have drinks parties or networking events for the exhibitors and a lot of business is done at these events. I know this fact to be true as it is, indirectly, how I came to be writing this book.

But what do you do if, frankly, you can't afford to exhibit yourself?

What worked for me was to volunteer my services to the networking organisation I was a member of at the time (4Networking) to help out on their stand. At the time, a lot of people didn't get why I would do this. 4N didn't pay me, it involved travelling to London and it meant being on my feet all day.

But I used these events not only to promote 4N, but to make contacts myself, people who in many cases I'm still in contact with now and have proven to be really useful connections along the way.

It was through attending and 'helping out' at the Great British Business Show that I met a commissioning editor from the *For Dummies* series and, ultimately, writing this book. The opportunities are there if you put in the legwork and look for them.

If you're a member of a networking group, or you're part of a business opportunity that itself exhibits at the show, consider offering your services to help out.

Feeling the Need for Speed Networking

Most of the shows, whether regional or national, have a networking element – often speed networking or something similar.

At a speed networking event, everyone gets to talk to every other person, one to one, but typically only for 2 minutes at each meeting, which, on the face of it, means that one person speaks for 60 seconds and then you swap.

If you're there and you run a business, which I presume you do as you're reading this book, you really may as well take advantage of the networking opportunity. It beats sitting on your own having a coffee and you never know what may come from it.

Speed networking, if you've never done it before, really is organised chaos. However, get in there and choose to enjoy it – speed networking can be noisy, energetic and, if you smile all the way through, fun.

 If you're going to go speed networking, remember to take lots of business cards. More so than in many other networking environments, everyone expects you to swap cards with them. These events are facilitated, often by a networking organisation, and someone is there to move you on to the next person, blow a horn or sound a whistle when it's time to swap over and generally be there to organise the chaos.

Doing something different

If you really want to win at a speed networking session, do something different.

Everyone else will talk about themselves. Everyone else will pitch at you about their business. Don't do that.

Instead, ask questions, scratch the surface a little bit about their business. Ask them whether they network anywhere else. Ask whether they'd mind connecting on LinkedIn.

Announcing your arrival

You can join up your social media and trade show networking by using this simple trick. If you're going to a trade show, find out whether they're using a particular hashtag for their twitter activity (for the Great British Business Show, it's #TBS2014). The obvious thing to do is broadcast that you're there using the hashtag (and you should do that too) but the less obvious, and much more productive, approach is follow the hashtag and then engage with anyone else who uses it. So someone tweets 'Really enjoying #tbs2014 and LOVED the @noredbraces seminar' and then you follow them and reply 'Hi, was gutted to miss that one; are you on one of the stands or a visitor here?' And then just have a conversation. You pick up new followers and massively increase the number of people you can follow up after the event.

And make notes. Whether you do so on the back of their card, take a notebook especially for the event or use Evernote or something similar, making notes is vital.

Following up

The very next day, you must follow up. You don't *have* to follow up anyone, although it's difficult to see a downside to doing so, but if anyone particularly clicked with you, connect with them on LinkedIn, or send them an email or card and resolve to keep in touch.

The connections and contacts you make at business shows are of no use at all unless you follow up sensibly. Someone should write a chapter about that.

Part II
Face-to-face Networking

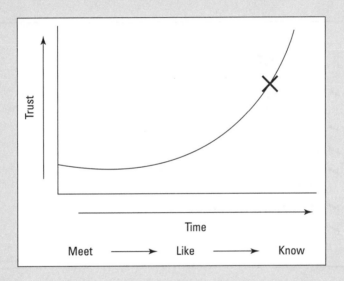

Go to www.dummies.com/extras/busines networking for free online bonus content about making the most of business networking.

In this part . . .

- ✔ Find out what to wear, what to take and what time to arrive to your business networking meetings.

- ✔ Calm your nerves before getting up to speak to the room.

- ✔ Discover what 'open' networking meetings are all about.

- ✔ Get the scoop on the introductions round – and stand out from the crowd.

- ✔ Identify how best to handle one-to-ones and follow-ups.

- ✔ Know what to do if you volunteer for the 10-minute speaker slot.

Chapter 6

Attending Networking Meetings

In This Chapter

▶ Ensuring that you're prepared for your networking meetings

▶ Ensuring that you *feel* prepared for your networking meetings

*I*n this chapter, I write as if you're about to attend your first networking meeting. I cover everything you need to do beforehand (you weren't just going to pitch up were you?) and right up to the point when you're ready to set off.

Even if you're a seasoned networker, this chapter is worth reading. You may find that some of the hints, tips and strategies are new to you, or it may just give you a refresher and a new sense of excitement about attending networking events.

Finding Time to Network

The UK offers plenty of networking options, which I explore in Chapter 4. There really is something to suit everyone, with every time of day covered, every format of networking and even gender-specific (typically female-only, although I have seen one or two male-only) networking events out there.

The thing is, not networking simply isn't an option if you want to succeed. No matter which business you're in, your competitors are out networking. For most businesses, the ability to have that human contact, to press the flesh and to make real some of those social media connections is far too valuable an opportunity not to take advantage of.

The world really is changing and the way in which you get your brand and your message out there is changing too. Word of mouth marketing has been turbo charged by social media. But word of mouth is still uniquely important. Having people who know you in 'real life' and who like and trust you makes a huge difference to all of your other marketing – even if you have a significant presence on the web.

So with options to network over breakfast, lunch and dinner (and I've even seen brunch, supper and drinks events), the question isn't *when* to go but *how often* you should be out there.

The more visible you are, the faster you build the relationships, the more your credibility among your crowd rises – plus, the more you find out about your own networking style.

The quickest way to build visibility and credibility is to immerse yourself in networking, in whichever format suits you.

Recognising that networking is real work

Sometimes when I talk to people about networking, they tell me they can't afford to take time out of their business to go networking. They talk about networking as if it's a luxury; something to be done when everything else in the business is taken care of. Frequently, people tell me that if their own business starts struggling, they'll go networking or when they've got through their current crisis and things are on the up again.

But what I've also noticed is that those people who get the most out of networking are those who seemingly spend loads of time out there, who are always networking somewhere and making new contacts. So have those people waited until they were less busy in their business? Or is it that their networking strategy is the thing which makes their business so successful?

In order to start making networking work, you need to start networking and you need to build networking into your working calendar.

If you begin by considering networking as part of your everyday work, then you'll always have the time and will always be building your network of contacts.

If you're wondering whether you have the time to go networking, think about the following: the networking pool potentially contains all of your contacts, prospects, suppliers and advisors for the future of your business. It may also contain new friends, social opportunities, opportunities for your business you haven't thought of and a future for your business you hadn't dreamed of. This question isn't about whether you have the time. Networking is where you should be spending your time. Networking is important for your business, if not vital for your business.

What does your business need? More clients, more customers, some advice, some support, a supplier of something?

What if I can show you a way of achieving all of that simply? Would you be interested?

Networking is talking to people. I bet that whatever your business needs right now, you can find what it needs by talking to the right people. You can find those people networking – directly, or by being introduced to them.

Networking *is* real work. You're at work when you're networking.

Networking to suit you and your business

Different businesses seem to exist at different times of the day. When I was an estate agent, it was vital that I was in the office first thing on a Monday as that was when the offers came in. It was equally vital that I was in on a Friday afternoon as that was when the *Oxford Times* came out and people would be calling in response to our advert in there (the Internet has changed all of that).

The plethora of networking options means that you can now build networking around your own work schedule without stressing yourself by feeling that you're missing the 'busy' period in the office. Look for networking opportunities that fit in with your existing schedule.

On top of that, many self-employed people have family commitments too and work their business around that. If you have school runs to do, you can choose a networking organisation that organises events in the middle part of the day or in the evening.

Have a look at your typical weekly schedule and build your networking around that. If your business is new, immerse yourself in networking until a pattern appears in your working week and then work within and around that.

Using your time twice

Do you have a business meeting to attend in another town?

I discovered early on in my networking 'career' how to use my time twice and look for networking opportunities that tied in with work commitments.

My work used to take me to Yorkshire often to work with one of my clients. Instead of just travelling to Yorkshire, doing the work and coming back, I would also look for networking opportunities while I was there.

I was already committed to being in that part of the country, and paying for the petrol to drive there and a hotel stay. I'd need to eat at some point so the only extra commitment arising from attending a networking event when I was there would be the extra few hours doing so.

But the potential rewards were huge. At the least I'd get to meet a few nice people, find out about their businesses and have the chance to tell them about mine. I'd even get some friendly company over breakfast, lunch or dinner.

What actually happened was that people were really interested in this guy from Oxfordshire who was networking so far from home. For that morning I was a bit of a celebrity, so people wanted to talk to me. I started going along whenever my business took me up there and, in time, some of the networking contacts turned into clients too. So then, every time I had to travel to Yorkshire for one client, I had other clients to see and networking events to attend.

Many successful business people talk about using 'leverage' –
in other words, making sure that for every hour of your day, for
every day of your week, you're making several things happen,
not just one.

For me, Yorkshire proved true leverage of my time. I took
the opportunity to meet other businesses, with the added
credibility that I was already in town on business.

Another way of using your time twice is when you need to
have a catch up or meeting with a client or supplier. I often
invite my clients along to a mutually convenient networking
event, and then hold our meeting straight afterwards. If your
client is attending this networking event for the first time, you
can make sure that you introduce them to other people who
may need their services – your client will *love* you for finding
other prospects for them!

If anyone cold-calls you and wants to meet up, invite them to a
networking event and have a meeting with them there. You won't
waste your time if what they're selling isn't of interest. They get
the opportunity to meet other prospects too and your networking organisation may even reward you for bringing a visitor. On
top of that, frankly, this method is a really neat way of dealing
with people who just seek to waste your time pretty quickly.

Get to the stage where your networking is so integrated into your
normal activity that it no longer feels like something extra.

Deciding What to Wear and What to Take with You

Preparation always helps you to feel better about attending an
event, or indeed anything you do in your business. Preparation
for attending business networking events is no different.

Making sure that you understand the dress code

I once attended an event in embarrassingly wrong dress.
I thought it was a casual event so turned up in chinos and a
polo shirt. Can you imagine how I felt when I walked in and
everyone else, *everyone*, was in a dark suit and tie?

Worse than that, we're English, so we're terribly polite and people welcomed me in and sat me down. I was in that room for four hours. Four hours wishing I'd phoned ahead and checked, or at least spotted everyone else while I was still able to turn round and walk away.

So phone ahead and ask; check with anyone you know who's going as to what people usually wear, if the event is formal or has a more relaxed dress code.

Thinking about the impression you want to make

Consider how you want to be perceived by others at the meeting.

A good course of action is never to judge anyone but presume that everyone else does judge people. I never judge people based on what they wear, but I know some people do and, while I'm completely confident wearing jeans and a flowery shirt to any event these days, when I first started I dressed to fit in with other people's expectations.

It takes more confidence at first to dress down than to dress up. Wearing a suit, or trousers and shirt for a man, or similar for a woman, is generally accepted 'uniform' and enables you to fit in and make a neutral impression on people.

Think about what's expected for your industry or profession too. If you're a banker, people expect you to be wearing a suit; if you're a window cleaner, probably less so.

Creative types – graphic designers, photographers, copy-writers and the like – can generally get away with being less formal than the professions too.

Jan Jack, a comedian based in the south of England, turned up for a networking meeting wearing pink pyjamas and fluffy slippers. It takes a lot of courage to really stand out like that but Jan created a huge impression, and continues to do so.

Many people feel more comfortable blending in; other people are happy to stand out. If you're at all unsure, start safe, particularly at your first meeting.

Being prepared with business cards – and plenty of them

Always make sure that you have business cards in advance. It may seem an obvious piece of advice but you'd be surprised how many people arrive without them.

Even in these technical times when all of our contacts are saved electronically, business people still expect that cards will be exchanged during a first meeting and, at some networking events, the exchange of cards is part of the agenda.

 If you're serious about your business, and you should be, spend a little bit of money on having your cards designed and printed. Having cards with 'Supplied Free by . . . ' printed on the back gives the impression that you don't care about your business enough to invest even a little bit of money in it.

Taking promotional material

If you have leaflets or brochures, find out in advance from the organiser whether you can put these out anywhere for people to take away.

If you choose to distribute leaflets, resist the urge to give one to everyone, or to put them on place settings – most people in the room won't be interested, plus it just comes across as pushy. Instead, display them in an appropriate place or just give them to those people who are actually interested in what you're doing. Networking events which allow you to display promotional material have a specific, and labelled, place for you to do so.

If you have a roller banner, ask the organiser if they'll permit you to put it up at the event. Roller banners can be a fantastic static advert for you and remind people of what you do and what your contact details are throughout the meeting.

 If you're likely to be the guest speaker at any event, take a roller banner with your contact and social media details on it so that people can record them easily throughout your presentation.

Knowing What Time to Arrive

In any networking organisation of any scale, you should receive a confirmation of your attendance and, particularly if you're attending for the first time, welcoming you and ensuring that you know the meeting format.

If, for any reason, you don't hear from anyone, get in touch to check these details for yourself, particularly if you're new to this group or this format.

Checking the meeting timings

Few things can embarrass you more than arriving halfway through a meeting (all right, lots of things are more embarrassing than that, but in the context of this book this eventuality is pretty embarrassing).

At one of the first networking meetings I attended, I managed to arrive halfway through the guest speaker slot. With everyone else sitting and listening, it was impossible to creep in unnoticed.

When you speak to the organiser in advance, check the start and end times and whether the meeting has a formal start time (in which case you need to be there for that time) or whether people can come and go during the meeting.

If you're going to a meeting or venue for the first time, allow more time than you think is necessary for you to get there. You may be travelling at a different time of day than usual for you and traffic may be heavier. If the event is in a large-ish hotel, you may take a little while to find the right room. Having a few minutes when you get there to compose yourself and do anything necessary before you go in is also really helpful, instead of rushing straight in from the car to the meeting (and spending the rest of the meeting wishing you'd had time to go to the loo . . .).

Entering as an early bird or fashionably late?

So, if the meeting has an advertised start time of 8:00 a.m., with the formal part of the meeting starting at 8:30 a.m., should you arrive at 7:45, 8:00 on the dot, or 8:25 just in time for the sit down bit?

Several schools of thought, as ever, exist on this matter.

The early bird catches the worm

Turning up early, just before the official start time, gives you significantly more time to network. You get the pick of the other attendees and plenty of time for conversation, small talk, and just getting to know the other people in the room.

If the meeting you're at has organised one-to-ones, you also have the opportunity to get yours booked up early with the people you want to speak to.

On top of that, that extra cup of coffee makes sure that you're wide awake when the meeting proper starts!

Fashionably late

I'll let you into a secret. I always used to get to networking events as late as possible to miss the 'open networking' part. These days I get there on time and have taught myself to enjoy it.

However, some people do see positive benefits from arriving there after everyone else has done their small talk. For example, people judge whether they want a one-to-one with you purely based on your introduction; you have less chance of being booked for one-to-ones by people who are less interested in what you have to say and solely interested in what they have to say.

You also have more time to prepare yourself mentally for the event if you need to.

Which to choose?

When you first attend a meeting, arrive at the stated time. If it says 8:00 a.m., aim to arrive pretty promptly at that time.

Over the next few meetings, you can get to see what time other people arrive and whether you can see any benefit to arriving particularly late or early.

Calming Your Nerves

You may not be nervous about attending networking events but I was and, to some extent, still am. I also speak to many people every year who are about to attend their first ever networking event and hear time and time again that they're nervous about it.

I remember, vividly, arriving for my first ever networking event and pulling up in the car park of the hotel it was being held in.

As I sat there, trying to sort out my head and my nerves, I managed to convince myself of a number of things:

- ✔ Everyone else in there will have a bigger business than me.
- ✔ Everyone else in there will have more money than me.
- ✔ Everyone else in there will have a better car than me.
- ✔ Everyone else in there will be more confident than me.
- ✔ Everyone else in there will be much more interesting than me.
- ✔ And so on!

You know when you've completely and utterly convinced yourself that something is true, even when you've absolutely no evidence to support your belief? That's what I was busy doing.

My head was pounding, I could feel myself going red and my stomach, well, my stomach wasn't being kind to me at all.

Before long I was ready to drive away and text some sort of lame excuse to the organiser and I know that some of you reading this chapter have done exactly that. I have friends in my own organisation who drove away the first time or had to be coaxed in by a friendly member who spotted them.

In truth, once I got inside, it was much friendlier and much more relaxed than I was expecting. The local members welcomed the new boy and made sure that I had somewhere to sit and people to talk to. I remember exactly who I was sat next to that morning and, before long, I was chatting to my neighbours at the table and starting to relax into the meeting.

I still know that most of you are more confident than me but I am willing to bet that a few of you nodded your head to my description above.

When I talk to people who are nervous about attending their first meeting, the nerves typically break down into a number of areas:

✔ They think that everyone else in the world somehow knows how to network and that they're going to feel foolish.

✔ The thought of walking into a room full of strangers is well outside their comfort zone.

✔ They're scared about standing up and presenting their introduction, even though it is only a few seconds long.

Knowing why your nerves may be your biggest asset

Feeling nervous is absolutely fine and normal; it's not disastrous and may even be helpful. Many rock stars and public speakers always feel nervous before they step up on stage.

I'm not going to tell you not to worry and that it'll be fine (although it will) because I know that doesn't help. Rather, I'm going to tell you how to work with the nerves, rather than try to fight them.

 Take five minutes away from reading this chapter and take a blank piece of paper and a pen. If you're terribly modern and trendy, you may want to take an iPad or similar tablet. (I accept that if you're that modern, you probably don't say 'trendy'.)

How does it feel when you're really nervous? Write down the physical symptoms for me. What actually happens to you?

✔ Churning stomach?

✔ Bit breathless?

✔ A little flushed?

✔ Maybe a tiny bit sweaty?

✔ Pounding heart?

Maybe you get other symptoms, too. Write those down as well.

Can you remember when you were last excited? What were the physical symptoms? Write those down too.

> ✔ Maybe you get a little flushed?
>
> ✔ Your heart beats faster than usual?
>
> ✔ You sweat a bit?
>
> ✔ You breathe faster?

When you've done this exercise, have a look at your two lists. Can I make a bet that they're pretty similar; that the 'symptoms' of excitement and blind terror are actually almost the same?

So who gets to decide which it is: nerves or excitement? Because from where I'm sitting they look pretty closely related physically.

A lot of performers manage to make that mental switch and know that what they're experiencing isn't nerves at all. It's the excitement and thrill of doing something new or performing in front of new people.

Have you ever felt more awake than you do when you're nervous or excited? The energy you feel when you're in that state is what a lot of performers use to propel their act and their presentation when they're on stage.

Your nerves and your physical reaction are your biggest asset as they keep you alert and energised throughout the meeting. Far better to be really wide awake than dozy and yawning!

Keeping on top of first-time jitters

Please know that everyone, just everyone, feels nervous the first time they attend a networking event.

Okay, so your mate Stevie is really confident and she just breezed through it and had a great time and she didn't feel like you at all and actually isn't it better that people like Stevie go networking and you just get back in your car and drive home?

Stop.

Almost everyone else felt nervous. It isn't just you.

Your biggest source of support is going to be what you've done before the meeting. Your preparation is vital to helping you feel more confident.

Rock stars don't get on stage without knowing exactly what they're going to play and having checked their instruments and kit out beforehand. Professional speakers have rehearsed what they're going to say over and over again (and most of us have a script hidden somewhere and a couple of well-rehearsed fall-back routines in case our nerves kick in).

So, how about a checklist of things to have ready the night before you go?

✔ Business cards in bag

✔ Introduction written and rehearsed and paper version in jacket pocket

✔ Suitable clothes out and ready

✔ Directions and/or sat nav postcode for the event jotted down

✔ Name of the organiser or person who offered the invite noted in phone

✔ Meeting timings checked and time allotted to travelling to event

✔ Meeting format re-read so it's familiar before setting off

This networking meeting may be really important to your business. Get an early night. Don't overdo it on the wine the night before (been there, done that) and have everything ready as if you were going to meet your biggest prospect ever, cos you never know, they may just be there.

Managing your nerves and appearing confident

I can still be nervous at an event and appear supremely confident. I've discovered several techniques and tricks along the way that help me get through.

If you're at a lunchtime or evening event, don't think that a glass or two of wine or a couple of pints will help your nerves. They'll actually make you go red in the face, sweat and breathe alcohol over people.

First, make every effort possible to arrive in plenty of time (whatever time you've chosen to arrive). You then have time to recheck everything before you go in and make sure that you're prepared, apply fresh lippy (as I always do) and get your breathing in check before you walk in.

If you have time in the car, close your eyes, allow your breath to slow down and simply spend two or three minutes just relaxing. If you know any meditation or relaxation techniques, now's the time to apply them. If not, just sit there quietly for a few minutes, enjoy being relaxed and try to look forward to the nice people you're going to meet.

If you have to have cash ready to pay for the event, get that to hand now, before you get out of your car, and have business cards easily accessible. That way, when you first walk in you won't be trying to locate your purse or wallet plus shake hands with the person you've just met and find a business card.

As you walk in, remember to smile. It really helps and people smile back at you, which also makes a difference to how you feel.

At most events, a good host welcomes any new guest or visitor and makes sure that you're eased in and introduced to people to talk to. If the host doesn't approach you, you'll find that by the time you've grabbed yourself a coffee and put your stuff down a regular will have said hello. I haven't been to a networking meeting yet where the existing members and regulars didn't warmly welcome the visitor.

If you're particularly prone to nerves and start to feel uncomfortable, simply excuse yourself, go to the toilet and spend a few minutes breathing and calming down.

As mad as it sounds, I run the cold tap and put my wrists under the water. A couple of minutes of that works wonders if I need to snap myself out of nerves.

Knowing what time to go home

So the meeting's over and it's time to leave.

You could, if you want to, just slip out unnoticed, leaving people wondering 'who that masked man was' (all right, more like 'man in smart casual clothing, I think he was called Steve and did insurance', but stick with me).

Or, you can take the last opportunity at this meeting to make a positive impression and get permission to take each relationship further.

Some of the above may come across as just common sense, but I'm surprised how many people don't do it.

If you enjoyed the meeting, go and tell the organisers and group leader. They're likely to be doing the role voluntarily. They'll see any positive feedback as welcome and at the same time you can ask what the protocol is for attending again and how you go about joining if you wish to.

If you enjoyed the speaker slot, tell her and tell her why as well. Be specific about what you enjoyed and what you found out. Ask whether she'd like to connect on LinkedIn or Twitter as well and then do so.

Thank the people you had one-to-ones with and reiterate however you've said you'll follow up.

Be the person who was remembered for being polite rather than just sloping off. Plus, you have the opportunity to make the organising team's day by telling them what you liked about the meeting.

Find something good to say. You can always think of something good, even if there were bits of the meeting you didn't enjoy. The people running it are almost always volunteers and appreciate your positive feedback but may be defensive if you're negative. Remember that you're there to build business relationships. Criticising what people are doing on your first meeting is unlikely to help that process.

Something else that this process does – it helps you to leave the event having reinforced to yourself what you enjoyed, what you discovered and what other positive benefit you got from the meeting – not a bad way to start your day.

Chapter 7

Making Connections in Open Networking

*A*lot of local events and 'sponsored' networking events are likely to be *open*, which means that they lack a formal structure.

Many people find these events intimidating but, with a bit of preparation, you can find it possible (and even easy) to network effectively – developing new contacts as you go.

In this chapter, I give you techniques and strategies to use in open networking environments wherever you may find them.

Understanding Open Networking

For me, the most frightening part of networking has always been the 'open' networking events, and the open networking part of many of the structured events. In short, open networking is simply networking without a structure. Think of open networking as a drinks party but with the goal of introducing yourself to other business people.

Mastering the skill of open networking is important because many networking events are simply open networking. If you learn how to use open networking effectively, you can use the same techniques in any environment where you find groups of people – whether these events are advertised as 'networking' or not. As well as the obvious networking environments, you'll also encounter corporate days out, seminars, industry get-togethers and many other events where these skills can prove extremely useful.

Introducing Yourself to People You Don't Know

Ultimately, open networking boils down to introducing yourself to people you don't already know. But how do you introduce yourself to someone you don't know, someone who may end up being your best ever prospect, referrer or supplier if you can only get to know them?

You'll get more from an event by setting yourself the goal of simply getting to know some people who you might be able to follow up with, rather than feeling that you have to achieve anything more tangible while you're there.

Put any thoughts of selling to the back of your mind and just go with the intention of making a few more relationships, a few more people who you never have to cold call.

Don't think of an open networking event as a card distributing exercise or a card collecting exercise. Each event is an exercise in adding a few more people into the 'Meet' and 'Like' end of the funnel.

Recognising that everyone's in the same boat

When I walked into my very first networking event, I managed to convince myself of a number of things.

First, I convinced myself that everyone else in the room, *everyone*, was more confident than me and somehow better at handling these events than me. I knew, deep inside me, that all these people would somehow be better business people – even though I didn't know what 'better' actually meant and certainly had no evidence to support that belief at all.

One of the biggest discoveries for me, which took me years to realise, is that most people in the room feel exactly the same as me. Those butterflies in your stomach? If you had X-ray vision, you'd see that most people at the event are going through exactly the same thing. Those trembling hands? If you looked closely (I don't recommend you do; it'd look weird) you'd see many people clutching their wine glass/coffee cup/ glass of water a little more tightly than is normal.

It's alright to be nervous! You're doing something outside of your comfort zone. That's okay. That's what a lot of business is about.

If you like, you can be incredibly liberated when you realise it isn't just you. Now we can look at some really simple techniques for making the event bearable and, if you want, even enjoyable.

Choosing who to approach

One of the oldest pieces of advice that still works is to get to the event early. If you're there before most other people, and you smile at the next person who comes through the door, they're likely to smile back and you can start a conversation.

If they don't smile back, they probably aren't worth knowing anyway, or perhaps need new glasses? You already have a referral for your local optician in the bag!

If you're not among the first there, then you're likely to walk into a room already full of people you don't know. So what do you do next?

You can, if you like, look for a person you know and go and chat to them. That's often been my preferred approach. But think this behaviour through. You've taken the trouble to go to a networking meeting, presumably to meet people you don't yet know, and yet you're talking to the one person in the room you *do* already know. The only way this works as a strategy is if you're sure that the person you know can introduce you to people who you don't yet know.

Instead, spend a few moments observing the other people in the room, which helps you decide whom to approach. You're unlikely to be in a massive hurry and you don't have to stand and stare; you can take a look around as you get a drink or get rid of your coat or whatever you need to do.

The following sections describe tried and tested techniques for choosing who to approach.

Targeting the loner

It may seem obvious, but is someone standing alone and looking nervous? They're not difficult to spot. Tell-tale signs are if someone is furiously staring at their phone or device, possibly looking as if they're terribly interested in an important text or email.

More likely, they just haven't read this book and don't know how to approach these events or how to introduce themselves to other people. They'll probably be extremely grateful if you approach them, as it saves them having to do it or standing around looking uncomfortable any longer.

Breaking into a group

What about if everyone is in a group? What about if there really are no wallflowers or people obviously alone?

You *can* break into a group but digging into a little basic body language before you do so is a good idea:

✔ If two people are facing each other, looking into each other's eyes, they're probably deep in conversation. The only polite way to approach them is to hover, making them aware you are there but not butting in until one of them invites you to do so. Even then, you may well be disturbing them discussing something that's important to them, so you joining them may not be welcome and they may be distracted with their stuff and not ready to pay attention to you. You aren't making a great start if you're seen as an interruption.

✔ If two people are standing at right angles, chatting but not facing each other, they're much more likely to welcome someone else into the conversation. Think about it as an incomplete triangle, where you can go and form the third side. This group is probably much more welcoming and you should feel comfortable just walking up and joining in.

✔ If three people are already in a tight triangle, you can treat them just as you can the two people facing each other. Presume that they consider their group to be closed and move on.

The networking dance

I read a blog recently which described the 'networking dance' and I thought it was worth repeating here as it makes a lot of sense.

You may be happily chatting to Brad when Lee walks up and hovers beside you. What's most likely to happen is that you open up your position with Brad to make space for Lee, who now joins the conversation. But then it doesn't become a three-way conversation; actually Brad and Lee are now chatting and you're a spare part. Thankfully, Lizzie walks up and you start chatting to her and the two couples separate and the whole process starts again.

So don't hesitate to walk up to a group and be ready to engage with the orphaned member. They'll thank you for it and you now have a grateful friend.

✔ If you see a group of three and only two of them seem to be talking, you can be sure that the third person can't wait to be rescued! They may have made the mistake of approaching the closed group of two people, in which case you can recommend this book to them so they can avoid the same mistake in future. (We do discounts for bulk orders, you know!)

Making an Impression

When you meet someone new, you want to make a good impression. Start by paying attention to your own body language. You may let it take care of itself when you're nervous and preoccupied but small details can make a huge difference.

The first, and most obvious and therefore most easy to forget, thing is to smile. Are people more likely to want to talk to the miserable git in the corner? Or the person who looks like they're happy to be there? Even if you grin like an idiot, people are going to want to know what's made you so happy. (Laughing to yourself isn't good, though.)

Consider what the following body language conveys about you:

✔ **Stand tall and proud.** Look confident. Walk as if you're confident. Be one of those people who other people are attracted to, talk to and want to find out about.

✔ **Stand up straight.** You simply look more appealing and confident when you do so. You'll also feel better if you adopt a confident pose.

✔ **Make eye contact as you approach people.** Simultaneously making eye contact and smiling at them is even better. And making eye contact, smiling at them and walking confidently and upright as if you know where you're going is even better still.

The handshake

When you've approached a person or a group, you then need to greet people and introduce yourself.

Fortunately, when deciding on how to greet someone when you meet them at a networking event, you have lots of approaches to choose from. You can shake hands, hug, fist bump, kiss on both cheeks or use other greetings I haven't even thought of. You can do nothing at all of course and just stand there and stare at the other person. Or maybe not.

A good old-fashioned handshake is the safest option by far. This act is universally accepted, you won't invade anyone's personal space and you won't cause offence.

I'm told, however, that people read a lot into how someone shakes their hand. When I was at school, we were taught how to shake hands in a job interview (and I remember watching two nuns shaking hands to demonstrate and finding it hilarious).

At many networking events, you wear a name badge. If you're a member of any of the networking organisations you probably have one. Always wear your badge on your right lapel or just above your right breast. This placement is the easiest place for someone to quickly look and read your name as they're shaking your hand.

What your handshake says about you

You may think that a handshake is a handshake but in fact you have several options, some of which are good and some that may leave an impression you didn't want.

Have a look at how you currently shake hands and what you may be conveying:

✔ If you offer your hand with your palm facing upwards, you're signifying submission and even subservience. While not necessarily a bad trait, it may not be how you want to come across the first time you meet someone.

✔ If you offer your hand with the palm facing downwards you're sending a strong signal that you want to be the superior partner in the relationship. You may want to demonstrate this superiority but be aware of how it appears if that is what you do naturally.

✔ If you twist the handshake so that the other person's hand now has the palm facing upwards you're not only signifying that you wish to be the superior partner, but also that you're prepared to control the relationship so that you are.

✔ Equally, pulling the other party closer to you signifies a need for control and you also run the risk of invading someone's personal space as they're most likely standing at a distance that feels comfortable to them.

✔ Squeezing too hard, as opposed to being firm, is never good. Actually hurting someone, even a little bit, on your first interaction is unlikely to create a good impression.

✔ Alternatively, not squeezing at all and giving a 'dead fish' handshake leaves exactly the impression that you expect it to – that you're weak and, potentially, disinterested in the other person.

✔ Have you ever seen how politicians shake each other's hands? As they shake with their right hands, the left hand grasps the forearm of the other person in a fake and insincere show of affection and friendship. Unless you know the person well, that's exactly how it comes across – insincere.

✔ Subtly touching the person's forearm with your left hand appears friendly and sincere. The line between the two is subtle, though, so only worth doing if you're confident that you're getting it right.

✔ Holding on for too long, unless you know the other person well, is likely to appear insincere and even a little threatening – a little like the person who forcefully pumps your hand up and down and leaves you to have to physically wrest your hand away from theirs. It's a little scary and weird and not really how you want to come across at first.

✔ At the other end of the scale, actually pushing someone away at the end of the handshake can easily appear unfriendly and cold.

Shaking the right way

In business, you're going to have to shake hands with people so you need to pay attention to how you do so.

So, if you want to get it right and come across as friendly but not clingy, confident but not controlling, do this:

1. **As you approach the other person, smile and maintain eye contact.**

2. **When you're a few feet away, extend your hand and your arm with your hand upright, palm facing sideways, and your thumb on top.**

3. **Presuming that the other person now proffers his hand in response, open your thumb and forefinger so that your hands easily glide together and grasp his hand so that your palms touch and your thumb and fingers wrap around his.**

4. **Subtly shake the hands, holding on for no more than a few seconds.**

5. **Pull your hand away, having created a confident and friendly first impression.**

For loads more tips, read *Body Language For Dummies* by Elizabeth Kuhnke (Wiley).

Starting a conversation

In addition to shaking hands, you also need to think of something to say. As a rule, standing there silently isn't likely to achieve much for either of you.

Before I wrote this chapter, I posed a question on a few Internet business forums asking what opening lines people liked using, and what really worked for them. I'd heard rumours, you see, that some magic words existed, certain phrases that would instantly build rapport and get the other party to warm to you.

And so, the most popular opener, used by some of the UK's most experienced networkers is . . . 'Hi'.

Now, I choose to do a little more than this, and I recommend that you do too.

Asking a question

Starting the conversation with a question will, of course, get the other person to respond. For example:

- ✓ 'Hi, I'm Stefan, and you are?'
- ✓ 'Hi, I'm Stefan. I don't think we've met before, have we?'
- ✓ 'Hi, I'm Stefan. Were you here last month (week/fortnight as applicable)?'

If you can see someone's badge, of course, you can instead say:

'Hi Sharon, I'm Stefan. What is it you do?'

Or:

'Hi Sharon, I've heard of XYZ Ltd but don't know what they do?'

Trying out opening lines

I've picked up some really clever opening lines from other people (who are as nervous about the whole thing as the rest of us), which I know are terribly effective.

If you're nervous, think about your openers beforehand and have a couple prepared that you can easily deliver and then let the other person speak while you catch your breath.

If you're at a loss for words, try one of the following techniques:

- ✓ Comment on the food – if the event you're at has a buffet, you've an ideal opportunity to talk to anyone! You can comment on the food, ask them about the food or, my personal favourite 'I'm missing out! Where do I find the buffet?'
- ✓ If you have a drink and the person you're approaching doesn't, you can offer to get them one. Nobody ever dislikes that as an approach and it always leads to further conversation.

✔ Recruit someone as an ally early on by saying, 'Hi, I've never done this before but you look like you have – can you tell me how the format works?'

When you're talking to someone, be fully there, in the moment:

✔ *Don't* look over their shoulder or glance around the room.

✔ *Don't* check your phone for messages.

✔ *Do* maintain eye contact.

✔ *Do* listen to what they say.

✔ *Don't* feign interest.

✔ *Do* be interested in the other person.

Answering 'So, what do you do?'

When you're chatting, your partner is soon going to ask, 'So what do you do?'

Make sure that you give this question some thought and have a few answers prepared. You've gone to the event to network, after all. You've got yourself out there not just to meet new people but so that people at least know that you and your business exist.

So you need to think this one through. Having plucked up the courage to walk up to someone, extend a warm handshake and engage them in conversation, you don't want to bring the conversation to a sudden end with a one-word answer.

'So, what is it that you do, Steve?'

'I'm a graphic designer.' Full stop. Period.

See, I know what graphic designers do. I also know what accountants do, what solicitors do, what web designers do and what many other professions, trades, industries and businesses do. If that's all you give me, I have you pigeon-holed with all the other graphic designers I've ever met.

So, add a tiny bit more colour, not only to keep the conversation going but also, and more importantly, to ensure that you're not lumped together with everyone else who does the same.

How about:

- ✔ 'We create brands and logos for small businesses.'

- ✔ 'Lots of small businesses get in a mess with their bookkeeping in the first few years. We help them sort that mess.'

- ✔ 'Nobody fully understands search engine optimisation. We make sure that our clients don't have to try.'

- ✔ 'We sell the houses that other estate agents can't sell.'

Walking in with a pizza box

A friend of mine, who wrote the foreword for this book, admits that he doesn't like open networking. In fact, he hates it and it makes him nervous. He much prefers the formal and structured part of networking meetings.

These days he's enjoyed a degree of success and is often recognised at business and networking events, but five years ago he was still building his reputation and profile and came up with a way to ensure that open networking was easier for him.

Part of Brad's story is that when he set up his first business, 4Consultancy, he was having to deliver pizzas at night to get cash in before the business took off. By the time 4Networking was established, this act had become part of Brad's presentation and has since become a big part of his written work.

We'd attend networking events and awards presentations for which 4Networking had been nominated and, while I did the nervous walking up and shaking hands thing, Brad would walk in with a pizza box under his arm.

Now trust me on this. If you walk into a room full of suited and booted people and you're carrying a pizza box under your arm, it isn't long before someone says words to the effect of:

'So, go on then, why are you carrying a pizza box?'

This, of course, gave Brad the perfect opportunity to say, 'Well, when I started my business I had to deliver pizzas at night to keep cash coming in. That's when I realised I needed a support network and set up 4Networking – have you heard of us?'

Now I reckon you had to have a load of confidence to do that, but Brad's experience was the opposite – it brought people to him, rather than him having to go to them.

All these are 'openers' that I've heard in real life, when I've met someone for the first time, and all have made me want to find out more.

Think about what it is you *do* rather than the name of your profession or trade.

Keep in mind that everyone is there to meet other businesses. That's the point of the event.

Chapter 8

Nailing the Introductions Round

*A*lmost all networking events have an introductions round, where all attendees take turns standing up and briefly introducing themselves and their business.

In this chapter, I talk about how you can make your introduction a success every time.

Getting the Scoop on the Introductions Round

I'm going to warn you now: if you go to a networking event, you *will* have to introduce yourself. I'm warning you because I don't want you to learn about the introductions round the hard way, like I did. (See the nearby sidebar 'What your introduction doesn't need to be like'.)

The introductions round is exactly what it sounds like: each person takes a turn introducing themselves and their business, one by one, to the entire group. In some organisations, the introductions round is called the 40-second round, or the 60-second round. In some places, you get longer or the time isn't measured at all.

What your introduction doesn't need to be like

I'm told that the part of business networking that people fear most is the introductions round. Don't I know it!

At my very first business networking event (Witney Big Breakfast), I almost couldn't deliver my 60-second introduction. Nobody had told me about that part of business networking so I was utterly unprepared. I only realised that I had to do an introduction when my friend Sharon stood up and introduced her business. To this day I can't remember what Sharon said, but I can remember that she was confident, had a perfect little speech and delivered it with well-rehearsed pitch and tone, with confident body language to add impact.

As Sharon sat down, the person next to her stood up and started delivering a presentation. This point is when it dawned on me that everybody in the room had to do it.

As we went round the table, the presentations were all equally confident and well delivered, or so it sounded to me. There were in-jokes with other people in the room, some people had props, and there were, inevitably, the painstakingly prepared straplines at the end, which everyone in the room already knew and joined in with.

As this activity was going on, I was making plans for how I could leave the room. I had nothing ready. I had no jokes, no funny strapline and no idea what I was going to say. And all of this embarrassment in front of a room full of other local businesses I wanted to impress.

Could I slip out and never come back? Difficult: there were only 16 or so of us and I would have been spotted.

How about pretend my phone was ringing with an emergency at home? I'm sure that I would have had one of those comedy moments when halfway through the imaginary conversation my phone would actually ring.

Or pretend to be ill? That could have worked.

Instead, with butterflies in my stomach, a red face and sweat pouring off me, when it got to my turn I stood up and mumbled a few words and sat back down again. I've never, ever been so relieved.

I'd very much like for everyone who reads this chapter not to have to feel like that.

 The point of the introductions round is to let other people in the room know what you do. Learning how to talk about and explain your business in short bursts is extremely valuable. The discipline of sticking to 40 or 60 seconds gives you the opportunity to really think about the important points and cut out the waffle. Use this experience as part of the value you get from business networking.

If the thought of an introductions round terrifies you, don't worry; you're not alone. The fear of public speaking is called *glossophobia* and researchers estimate that 75 per cent of people suffer from it at some point (presumably the point at which they're about to stand up and talk).

Many professional speakers and even pop stars get some degree of anxiety before they perform and have methods and strategies to deal with it. One of the best strategies is to be prepared. This chapter can help!

Remembering that you're trying to get the interview, not the job

You may think of your introduction as your opportunity to tell everyone in the room about every service you provide, when you started the business, where you're based, what qualifications you have and even what special offers you have on this month.

Stop.

You aren't going to sell someone your product or service in 40 seconds. So stop trying. It may even take some of the pressure off you to realise that you don't have to try to sell to everyone as you stand there.

 The point of the introduction is to get the interview, not the job. You don't want to have people queuing with order forms, but to have people queuing for a one-to-one (which I cover in Chapter 9). The point of the introduction is to attract enough interest from other people in the room that some of them want to continue the conversation afterwards. So relax, be you, and allow people to see that you believe in what you do.

Avoiding the elevator pitch error

The *elevator pitch* goes along these lines: you get into a lift and the only other person in there is Richard Branson. You have that once in a lifetime chance to tell him about your business and why he should invest in it or at the very least hire your services.

But trauma! Richard is only going up two floors. You have less than 60 seconds and have to impress him in that time. You have to give him enough in that 60 seconds to make him sign a cheque there and then!

The elevator pitch is what you say in that situation. Perfectly crafted so that in less than a minute you not only excite your prospect's interest but you get that person to such a fever pitch that they immediately want to do business with you.

But you're not going to meet Richard Branson in a lift! And even if you did, he'd most likely be thinking about something else. And even if he wasn't, he may not need what you have to offer. And even if he did, is he really going to buy from someone who chased him into a lift?

The problem with an elevator pitch, or any other sort of set script to sell your stuff, is that the other person doesn't have the script. And people simply don't buy services from strangers if they don't absolutely have to.

The introductions round has often been likened to everyone doing an elevator pitch and many people do that. Hopefully, everyone else in your networking room will do an elevator pitch, while, having read this book, you stand up and deliver something better.

The elevator pitch presumes that the people around you care about your business and are already listening. The likelihood is, and a better presumption to make at least, is that everyone else in the room is there for the sake of their business and not yours.

If you adopt the elevator pitch approach, you're – in effect – answering the wrong question. People aren't yet interested in what you do and how you do it.

The question that people want answered isn't what you do but what they can get from working with you. If you can answer that in your introduction, you can get significantly more interest from the other people in the room.

Standing Out from the Crowd

If you want to stand out from the crowd, you need to get to know what's expected during the introductions round because some organisations have a structure they prefer you to stick to, while other organisations and networking groups allow you to do whatever you like in your introduction.

For example, if your networking group is a referral-based setup, then the format is more likely to be about explaining who you are, what your business does and what type of referral you're looking for that week.

Think about this, though. Do you want to be one of the crowd, or do you want to stand out among the others? If people have sat through 15 or 20 near identical pitches, why not try something different?

Instead of spending hours trying to come up with a memorable strapline to sit among all the other memorable straplines, why not come up with a truly memorable introduction?

If you're already attending networking meetings, have you ever sat there during the introductions round, not listening to the others but planning what you're going to say, or mentally rehearsing your own introduction, or deciding who you want a one-to-one with? Guess what? That's what other people are doing too, while you're doing your introduction. So the key is to give them something to make them prick up their ears, pique their interest and have them wanting to find out more.

Preparation, preparation, preparation

When I was in estate agency, we used to advertise every week in the local paper to show off our services in the local community. It cost us a fair bit of money and we used to spend time putting the ad together. I spent nearly 20 years in estate agency and we never once waited until the last minute to rush some text together.

And yet people invest their money in membership of networking organisations, get up early to travel there, take time out of their day and don't prepare what they're going to say. Instead, with the opportunity to communicate with people who may need their services, who are for that 40 or 60 seconds a captive audience, people wing it with no preparation or thought given to what they're saying.

The introductions round is your opportunity. You've already invested the money and the time to be there. Now is your chance to maximise that opportunity and engage people in wanting to find out more.

Preparation really is the key to success and gives you the opportunity to think about the main points of your service or product that can grab people's attention.

Preparation also helps you feel and sound more confident. If you know exactly what you're going to say, you can concentrate on how you deliver, how you use your voice, your body language and your presence to give your message impact.

Think about what they might be buying, not what you're selling

What do you *really* do? Not what you think you do, not what it says on your business card, but what you actually do?

I've heard far too many people just say the name of their profession: 'I'm David Smith and I'm an accountant.' Put thought into what makes you unique. Other accountants exist. No matter what you do, I promise you other people do the same. I've yet to meet a completely unique business and I meet hundreds of businesses a year. (If your business is honestly unique and nobody but nobody does the same as you, tweet me and tell me @NoRedBraces!)

Don't be tempted to trot out the same unique selling point (USP) as everyone else in your industry:

- ✔ 'We pride ourselves on our customer service' (I've yet to hear any business saying 'we're rubbish at customer service'!)

- ✔ 'We offer fantastic value for money' (well, you should, the alternative is pretty rubbish!)

Get creative; think about what you do that others in your industry or profession don't. Here are a few great USPs I've heard to get you thinking:

- ✔ A firm of builders that guarantees they'll arrive when they said they would – and give you £50 if they're late.

- ✔ A bookkeeper who gives you a monthly freepost envelope to stick your receipts in to return them.

- ✔ An IT support company that charges one low monthly fee.

- ✔ A sales specialist who only charges you if you sell more after working with him.

Stop reading now. Get a blank piece of paper. What have your clients said about you that makes you truly unique? What do you do that makes you stand out among others in the same business? What is it about your business that means people should talk to you?

I've heard far too many people describe themselves as a 'boring' accountant, or insurance specialist, and so on. Unless you can really ham it up and make an act out of being boring in 60 seconds, don't do it. Don't demean yourself or the profession you spent years studying for.

You're not in competition with the other people in the same business; there's plenty of business for everyone. But you *are* in competition for people's attention in a busy world and a busy environment.

Using soundbites

Towards the end of my estate agency career, I specialised in selling what we called 'probate sales'. Put simply, this specialism meant properties that had been left in a will after someone had died.

In order to truly specialise in this field, I needed a decent understanding of probate law. I needed to understand and be clear about who the client was (not as obvious as it seems) and when we could start selling the property. I needed a good grasp of local planning law as this type of property often lent itself to redevelopment.

But if I explained all of that when I first met people, their eyes would (quite rightly) glaze over. *How* you do what you do is of no interest to others at the introduction stage. But the *effect* of what you do is.

Consider what soundbites you can build around your business. What describes your business in a way that's easy to understand for the people listening?

In my case, I had letters and emails from clients thanking me and saying how *I'd achieved much more for the sale of their property than other estate agents had valued it at.* That's what people needed to know. That was my soundbite. That was what I made sure that people knew about me.

This soundbite had two effects:

✔ It made it easy for the person I was talking to to understand what I did.

✔ I could use the soundbite to put my business into a little box I could hand to someone else and they'd instantly understand the value and benefit of working with me.

Having a soundbite helps you to sell 'through' the room as well as 'to' the room, because your contacts can easily pass on your soundbite to their contacts.

Using props

If you think that introducing props into your introduction adds weight to it, or explains something simply, then do it. Props can be a brilliant attention grabber and give people something else to remember you by.

Do make sure that your props are relevant to what you do and bring something to the introduction, rather than confuse the other people in the room.

Some examples that have worked well include:

✔ A bookkeeper who held up a torn supermarket carrier bag full of receipts and asked, 'Does your bookkeeping look like this?'

✔ An IT support specialist who carried a toy tortoise, explaining that the tortoise has survived over millions of years doing everything it does as slowly as possible to conserve energy. Then he said 'Your PC is meant to work very fast. If it's moving as slowly as the tortoise – call me!'

If you can come up with a prop that really adds to your presentation, you can become not only memorable but also talked about: 'Have you seen the guy who carries the tortoise?', 'Have you seen Sue the bookkeeper and her bag of receipts – it's really funny!'

Be creative and consider using a prop if you can make it work.

Understanding body language

When you deal face to face with someone, over 55 per cent of the emotional message comes from your non-verbal communication, in your body language and how you say what you say.

Your body language conveys a message whether you're consciously doing so or not. You don't have a choice over whether other people read and subconsciously interpret your body language (they will) but you do have a choice over whether you take some control of it.

When you're standing in front of a group of people, being aware of your body language can make a massive difference to how confident you look and feel. The two are, of course, linked.

If, after reading this section, you'd like more of an understanding of body language, then I strongly recommend *Body Language For Dummies* by Elizabeth Kuhnke (Wiley).

Stand up!

Firstly, and possibly most obviously, you need to stand up. I've been to networking events where some people, sometimes even most people, delivered their introduction sitting down. I still stand up. So should you.

Singers stand because doing so elongates the body, gives more room to breathe and allows them to use their voices more powerfully. Teachers stand to make themselves the focus in the room and give them authority over their students. The combination of these benefits is what you're looking for.

I thoroughly recommend that you rehearse your body language just as you rehearse the content of your introduction.

Stand away from the chair or table. Unless you have a medical condition, you don't need anything to support you and you'll feel more confident (even though you may think the opposite is the case) if you stand up and support yourself. Standing away from the chair also makes a step towards removing a barrier between you and your audience. In a busy room standing far away may be difficult, so just step back as far as possible.

What you want to have perfected in your rehearsals is your stance, so that you can step into it straight away when your turn arrives.

How do you stand when you're feeling confident? How would you stand if someone wanted to take a photo of you in a confident and strong pose? Picture you at your most confident, presenting with ease to the people in the room.

Now stand like that!

Starting with your feet, find a position with your legs slightly apart where you feel rock solid. Think of the roots of an oak tree keeping the tree rooted (literally) to the ground. Allow your body weight to rest completely on both feet.

If I were to come up to you now and push gently, would I be able to unsettle you or would you remain rock solid? Find the position where you feel completely solid. Stand like that.

Standing up straight, you look and feel more confident and this position makes it easier for you to breathe (which you still want to do!). Take a look at Figure 8-1 for a confident stance.

Your arms

Crossing your arms in front of you is almost universally regarded as defensive. You're using your arms to hide behind, very literally. Have a look at Figure 8-2 – does this stance look defensive to you? Not how you want to come across in your introduction! You've nothing to hide, so uncross them.

Figure 8-1: A confident and rooted stance.

A perfect starting position for your arms is by your sides or held in front of you with your hands loosely clasped.

Completely opposite to the arms folded position is the arms open position, which conveys openness, honesty, friendliness (you don't have your 'shield'; you trust the other person) and having nothing to conceal, as shown in Figure 8-3.

Your face

Make sure that your face is also presenting the right image. So smile! You're happy to be there. You're happy to have the opportunity to introduce your business to the other people in the room. They won't just be able to see your smile; they'll hear it too.

Allow brief eye contact with a few people in the room as you speak and smile at them; they'll smile back and pay more attention.

Figure 8-2: This stance may feel comfortable and 'safe' for you, but look at how it looks to those you're trying to impress.

Practise your body language

Practise your body language in front of the mirror. My own smile unnerves me when I see it looking back at me, but at least I know how to do it.

The easiest and simplest way to boost your confidence for the introductions round is to change your own body language. Stand confidently and let your face show that you're happy to be there. The rest will follow.

Can you hear me?

As well as strengthening your message with your body language, you can use your voice to ensure that your message is heard. I don't just mean speaking loudly, though.

As you stand up, take a deep breath right into your diaphragm. Once again, practise this breath to know how it feels to you.

Figure 8-3: Arms open and welcoming.

When you're nervous, your voice tends to speed up. You want to ensure that people can follow what you're saying, so just take a breath and consciously slow yourself down.

Speak clearly and with enough power in your voice that everyone in the room can hear you. Bear in mind that during a networking meeting you hear background noises; people chinking their plates and cutlery, people moving their own notes around as they mentally practise their introduction, coffee and tea cups being lifted and put down and even the odd whisper between individuals.

Don't be the one whispering. The whisperer is being *really* off-putting and disrespectful to the person speaking, and conveys the message, 'I'm more interested in what I have to say than what you have to say.' Not a great message for networking.

Injecting your introduction with passion and confidence

You want people to believe in you and be confident in the service or product you provide. You want people to be interested enough in what you've said in your introduction that they want to find out more and ask you for a one-to-one.

This belief and confidence needs to come from within you. Use your tone of voice to convey to everyone else just how excited and confident you are about what you have to offer. (If you really aren't passionate and confident about your business, please go and find the thing you *are* passionate about and go and do that instead!)

The way to demonstrate this confidence is (again!) preparation. Make sure that you have an introduction that you can present confidently. Practise it in front of the mirror a few times to get used to saying it and start to fix it in your memory.

Most phones these days have a voice recording function and this function really is your friend when you're practising your introduction. How do you sound? Are you happy with it? Practise over and over again until you're comfortable with your introduction, remembering the tone and inflection you put on each phrase and word.

Rules to Follow and Things to Avoid

Some things that people say or do (or sometimes don't say or don't do) that can really make or break their introduction include the following:

- ✔ Other people in the room may offer similar services to you. Don't say, 'We offer a similar service to Steve who spoke earlier.' Instead, concentrate on the positive and unique features of what you do.

- ✔ Don't knock the competition. Ever. You'll find out that someone in the room is the brother of the competition you're knocking. In any case, knocking the competition never sounds positive.

✔ Stick to the meeting's timings. If the introduction is supposed to be 60 seconds, do *not* be the person who goes on well past that. People will stop listening and wonder what's so important about what you've got to say when they all stuck to the timings, and your message will be lost.

✔ Being able to present your business concisely and with impact is a really valuable skill. Trying to be clever and taking up more time just won't help.

✔ You're probably not a professional comedian. Something that's incredibly funny in your head may fall flat if you try to weave it into your introduction. Stick to talking about your business.

✔ If you run more than one business, avoid talking about them all in the same introduction. Someone who says they 'wear several hats' can sound as if they're a jack of all trades (and a master of none), even though many entrepreneurs run more than one enterprise at a time. Concentrate on the product or service that will encourage people to speak to you; they can find out about your other services as the relationship develops.

Introducing Sample Templates for Your Introduction

At least at first, the introductions round is easier if you have a template, or structure, to work from.

The most memorable stories and speeches follow structures that work. The stories you remember the most follow a structure and form.

Ever watched a Pixar film like *Toy Story* or *Cars*? Every one of them follows a set structure, designed to make them memorable:

'Once upon a time_____. Every day_____.
One day_____. Because of that, _____.
Because of that,_____. Until finally_____.'

Don't believe me? Here's *Finding Nemo* in less than 100 words:

Once upon a time there was a fish called Nemo whose father, Marlin, was extremely protective of his son. **Every day**, Nemo listens to his father warning him how dangerous the ocean is and imploring him not to swim too far away. **One day** Nemo decides to ignore Marlin and swim farther than he should. **Because of that**, he becomes prey to a diver collecting fish for a collector. **Because of that**, his father sets out to rescue him. **Until finally** Nemo is reunited with his father and discovers that trust is a very big part of love.

There you have it. (I still prefer the film to my version, though.)

Luckily, you only have 40 or 60 seconds to fill but, even then, that brief time can seem an eternity if you forget your story and lose your way.

Using a template helps you put some form around the introduction and that makes it easier for you to remember what you're saying next.

Every great presentation, like any great film, has a defined beginning, middle and end and each of the templates I suggest has that.

The attention grabber

Say you're the 23rd person to do your introduction in a room of 25 people. Most people in the room now have 40-second fatigue from listening for approaching half an hour to other people's introductions. Most people have breathed a sigh of relief that they've got their introduction over with, decided who they want a one-to-one with and started wishing it was time to grab another coffee.

You don't even get the benefit of being the last in the room when everyone pretends to be attentive again; a bit like at the end of a church service. Don't pretend you haven't done it!

The point of the attention grabber is to get people to notice you, to rise from their slumber and focus on what you're saying.

The structure

The attention grabber goes something like this:

1. **Stand up.**
2. **Headline.**
3. **Introduce who you are and what you do.**
4. **Tell them how you do it.**
5. **Call to action.**
6. **Sit down again.**

The headline

Typically, people start with introducing themselves. In this structure, you start with a headline. The headline is designed to wake people up so that by the time they get to Step 3 (who you are), they're already listening.

The headline itself can take several forms. I used to open with a question: *'Would you like to win more business using business networking?'*

If you're going to ask an opening question, it needs to be a closed question; that is, the answer can only be 'yes' or 'no' and you need to phrase it so that the only possible answer is 'yes'.

So don't ask:

- ✔ 'How would you like to . . . '
- ✔ 'What is the . . . '
- ✔ 'Is there anyone in the room who . . . '
- ✔ 'Who wants to . . . '

And do ask:

- ✔ 'Would you like to . . . '
- ✔ 'Have you ever . . . '

As you finish the question that needs a yes answer, stick your hand up in the air, like when you wanted to answer a question at school. This gesture grabs people's attention and leads to people agreeing with you.

I've also used a bold headline: *'Business networking does NOT work!'*

Whatever you use as a headline, remember the point is to grab people's attention so they can't help but take notice of you.

The introduction

Step 3 is the introduction itself with *who* I am and *what* I do: 'My name is Stefan Thomas of No Red Braces and I help people to win more business from business networking.'

Yours might be:

- ✔ 'I'm Sharon Swanston of SS HR Services and I keep business people on the right side of employment law.'

- ✔ 'I'm Nauris Petrovich of Premier Financial Services and I help people protect their incomes, their families and their savings from any unexpected changes in their lives.'

- ✔ 'I'm Lee Rickler of Point and Stare Online Development Agency. I make sure that my clients are proud of their websites and know that they're presenting their business in the best possible light.'

- ✔ 'I'm Graham O'Leary of Making Sense of Numbers and I ensure that clients not only understand their bookkeeping and accounts but also how to use those numbers to win more business.'

The how-you-do-it

Step 4 expands into *how* I do it:

- ✔ 'I work with people one-to-one, or in small groups around the country, and make sure that my clients feel confident when they tell people what they do, using language that's exciting, concise and compels people to want to find out more.'

- ✔ 'I become a part of my clients' teams, working alongside them and taking the stress of HR away, leaving them to concentrate on their core business.'

- ✔ 'My clients tell me what's worrying them financially, and I help them stop worrying by working out a unique plan for them.'

Maya Angelou famously wrote, 'People will forget what you said; people will forget what you did; but people will never forget how you made them feel.' This statement has huge relevance to your introduction. Notice that the examples talk about taking stress away, stopping people worrying, giving people confidence. These kinds of things are much more interesting to someone than your qualifications or where your office is based. People buy with their emotions and want to find out more when you tell them the emotional benefit of your service.

The call to action

Step 5 is a call to action.

On any piece of marketing material you use – your website, any leaflets you have, your pop-up banner, any advertising you do – you're likely to have a call to action; something that instructs people on what to do next if they want to find out more. This call to action may be phoning you, filling in a form for more information or the perennial furniture store favourite: 'OFFER ENDS SUNDAY – DON'T MISS OUT'.

Considering your introduction is part of your marketing material, it makes sense to include a call to action.

I always use something along the lines of: 'If you want to find out more, ask me for a one-to-one' (which also works in the spirit of using your introduction to sell people on the idea of having a one-to-one with you).

Try:

- ✔ 'You'll find details on my website: 4Networking.biz.'
- ✔ 'Please take one of my leaflets, which has full details.'
- ✔ 'To enrol for the course, simply see me afterwards and I'll take your details.'

Make it clear to people that, if they like what they hear, they can find out more by following your call to action.

Putting it all together

So a full attention-grabber introduction goes along these lines:

'Do you want to understand social media – Twitter, Facebook and LinkedIn – so that you get a steady stream of real, qualified enquiries for your business?

I'm Steve Martin of Engaging Social Media and I make sure that my clients have a social media strategy which delivers real business.

I achieve this by working with them or their marketing teams to ensure that they're confident their social media both conveys the right message and provides a simple, hassle-free method of following up on every lead (including the many that may not even be addressed to you).

If you'd like to find out more, I'm running a free introductory session next Tuesday. Ask me for a one-to-one and I'll book you in.'

By the way, I time that at around 35 seconds. The speech is powerful, concise and leaves your listeners wanting to find out more.

The third-party endorsement

Imagine how fantastic it would be if you had a few of your most satisfied clients in the room. At the relevant moment, they could stand up and tell everyone how brilliant you are and what a positive difference you made to their business or life.

The next best thing is to use the nice things your happy clients have said about you.

The structure

The third-party endorsement introduction is structured as follows:

1. **Stand up.**
2. **Tell them who you are.**
3. **Tell them what you do.**
4. **Tell them how you do it and the effect that it has on your clients.**
5. **Give a short testimonial from a client.**
6. **Tell them who you are again.**
7. **Sit down.**

This structure sits more comfortably with some people who have told me that people are expecting to hear who the speaker is as the first point, and that when they do so that starts off the 'trust' part of the relationship.

All about you

In Step 2, you say something like, 'Hi, I'm Cara Maneer from Onyx Marketing Services.'

Speak clearly and confidently; be proud of your business, and let your listeners hear it in your voice.

Steps 3 and 4 follow the same structure as the attention- grabber template, earlier in this chapter.

Testimonials

Step 5 gives you the opportunity for a third-party endorsement.

Third-party endorsements work a bit like this. Everybody expects you to say that you're brilliant. You're the biggest advocate and evangelist for your business and if you're excited about your business you want that to come across in your introduction.

But that's what everybody expects. Somebody else, an independent third party, saying you're brilliant; now that's a whole lot more powerful.

A short third-party testimonial sounds something like this:

- ✔ 'James Worley of Insect PC said that I was the first marketing consultant, in over seven years of trading, who truly understood what Insect PC did and how to communicate that.'

- ✔ 'After working with Belinda Patel at BJ Photographs for six months, she more than tripled her turnover, solely as a result of using the techniques I taught her.'

- ✔ 'I looked at Osborne and Sons car dealership and was able to save them £17,000 per year on their utilities – they've ploughed this month's saving straight into an advertising campaign, which led to a 300 per cent increase on their sales.'

Make it real. Have a look at your LinkedIn recommendations and testimonials on 4Networking or other sites. What have people said that's useful to you? Do you have letters or emails from clients which you're keeping to yourself at the moment?

You don't need permission to use recommendations and testimonials because you're simply reading out what somebody has written about you.

As well as being a powerful endorsement of your services, a third-party endorsement does something else when you use it in networking. It may be the thing that has someone else in the room thinking, 'I know Osborne and Sons; their building is about the same size as mine. I wonder if I can save that much?' Or 'Blimey, I thought Belinda was doing all right anyway; I wonder what this guy knows that has helped her so much?'

Using a third-party testimonial takes your service from being an abstract concept and makes it real. Relating to real people brings the concept alive in people's minds.

Only ever use testimonials from real people, preferably people who are local and may be known to others in the room. Saying that you once worked with some guy in a different country who had fabulous results doesn't sound believable. Don't ever, ever make up a testimonial.

Putting it all together

A third-party endorsement introduction goes something like this:

> I'm Stef Thomas of No Red Braces and I help people build structure and story into their presentations, so that when they stand up to present, they do so confidently, knowing exactly what to say and how to deliver their message with passion. If you want to find out how, buy *Business Networking For Dummies* from me, which has 25 five-star reviews on Amazon and was reviewed in *The Oxford Mail* as being 'an invaluable and inspiring guide, and also great value'.

> So please see me, Stef Thomas, for a one-to-one to see how you can improve your presentations and bring in the business you deserve.

See? It works.

Remembering What You Planned to Say

A fallacy held by many people is that you can remember things when you're feeling nervous or under stress. If you've never had that 'rabbit in headlights' moment when speaking in front of other people, you're lucky.

Have you ever seen those out-take programmes on TV of footage of famous actors and newsreaders forgetting their lines and swearing or descending into giggles? Most professional speakers and actors keep some sort of memory aid around them; something to continually remind them what to say next, or to help out in an emergency if they're distracted or their mind goes blank.

You don't have the benefit of being able to do a second take of your introduction, so here are a few pointers to make sure that you remember what you're going to say:

✔ Write down your presentation word for word and get used to reading it out aloud. If something doesn't sound right when you say it (even if it sounds great in your head), you can always change it.

✔ Practise a few times in front of the mirror, considering your body language and tone of voice as you do so.

✔ If you've recorded yourself on your phone's voice memo facility, listen to the recording several times to help you 'fix' the presentation in your memory.

✔ Another really great use of your mobile phone is to time yourself. You'll know ahead of time whether your favoured networking organisation allows 40 seconds, 60 seconds or something different for the introduction and you can ensure that your presentation, spoken aloud, fits within that.

✔ If you're really nervous, take the word-for-word speech with you and read it out loud. Nobody in the room will mind. Nobody expects you to be an expert public speaker.

Once you're used to the words and the feel of your introduction, you can put the major points in order on a small card that you can easily carry around with you and use as a prompt.

Print the major points in a large font so that you can still read the card if you leave it on the table as you stand up. You don't have to look at it all the way through but you can be confident knowing that the prompt is there if you need it.

Mixing it up

Whether your networking group has the same people every week or you regularly speak to a different set of people, make sure that you have two or three introductions up your sleeve:

✔ Mixing it up prevents you from getting bored with the same thing every week, which you may inadvertently convey to your audience.

✔ Introducing different testimonials or different facets of your service

may help the penny to drop with someone in the room and encourage them to speak to you.

✔ If someone in the room offers a similar service to you, you can vary what you say in case they say similar things to you.

✔ You'll find it great practice to think about all the positive benefits of your service and revisit some of the testimonials you've received.

Chapter 9

Handling One-to-Ones

● ●

In This Chapter

▶ Understanding the point of one-to-one meetings in networking

▶ Choosing who to have a one-to-one with

▶ Knowing what to say (and not to say)

● ●

*Y*ou may think that you know what someone does, from listening to their introduction, or looking at their brochure and website. But really getting to know someone takes a little more time. The point of the one-to-one meetings in networking terms is to open your relationship a little further and enable you to find out not only about your contact's business, but also to get to know them as a person.

Getting the Scoop on One-to-Ones

Ditch the jargon. A one-to-one is simply a conversation with someone else from your networking circles. Whether or not your networking group has formal one-to-ones, getting to know other people in business helps you develop relationships.

The phrase 'one-to-one' can mean slightly different things. Different networking groups have different 'rules' around how and when to have a one-to-one with another member.

At BNI, for example, a one-to-one is to be conducted between networking meetings, arranged privately between members. At 4Networking, in contrast, the one-to-ones happen within the meeting time.

Ignore all the rules for a second. If you're sensible, you'll get to know more about other people in the room and their businesses. The more you know about them, the more you may find you like them, realise that your business has something to offer them or them to you, and the more likely you are to be able to refer business to them when the opportunity arises.

Making one-to-ones a regular part of your networking helps you to move every relationship from just knowing the person based on their introduction, to having a much deeper understanding of them and their business.

Having a one-to-one with everyone

If you're worrying about who to speak to, whether they're the right contact for you, likely to know the right people, or if you'll benefit from spending your time having a one-to-one with them, stop.

Now. Just stop.

I don't want to sound like a hippy but open your mind. You've no idea what value the other people in the room have to you until you start actually getting to know them. The fact that they're in an industry completely unrelated to yours has no bearing on whether you should get to know them better. The fact that you already buy the service they offer from another provider makes no difference to whether they know people who might be perfect to talk to you. The fact that they actually do the same as you doesn't mean that you can't collaborate.

Instead of expending mental energy working out who you should get to know, why not expend the same energy getting to know everyone and see where each relationship leads? Some may lead to nothing but you still have a warm contact who you can pick up the phone and talk to.

Even if you don't like or get on with the person you've had a one-to-one with, at least you now know that and know you won't do business with them in the future.

Getting the Most from One-to-Ones

Before you consider what you want to achieve from any one-to-one, I want you to put any thoughts of selling to the back of your mind. If you put yourself under pressure to sell, that's going to come across and may resemble desperation, which isn't a good look.

If you don't try to sell, you have more opportunity to find out about the other person and their business without constantly looking for opportunities to tell them about your stuff.

So what would you like to achieve from the one-to-ones you have?

A sensible outcome is to look for something that you have in common with the people you meet – some shared experience or passion that gives you something to talk to them about when you meet. Or you may find out that an individual is someone who doesn't do small talk, so you can respect that in future and, if you ever have the opportunity to introduce your services, can do him the courtesy of getting straight to the point.

Where to have a one-to-one

If you're organising one-to-one meetings outside of the networking group, think about where to have them.

Surprisingly, at your office or theirs isn't likely to be the right place for your first meeting for a couple of reasons:

- One of you is 'in charge' as the other is on your territory.
- You may be distracted by emails coming in, phones ringing and colleagues interrupting.

Instead, consider having your first one-to-one meetings on neutral territory.

Co-working spaces are absolutely ideal for your first informal meeting with someone. They're utterly neutral territory. They usually have comfortable chairs, and desks so that you have the opportunity to make notes straight afterwards. They usually provide free tea and coffee.

Other sensible places to meet are

✔ **Hotel lobbies.** Hotels are easy to find, usually have parking and some of the new breed of modern hotel, such as Village Resorts (`www.village-hotels.co.uk`), have plenty of open space and seating for business people to meet informally.

✔ **Coffee shops and cafes.** Check beforehand that they aren't too busy and/or noisy to carry on a conversation.

A pub isn't the best place to have a first meeting with someone. You have to deal with the little social game of deciding whether an alcoholic drink is appropriate, the potential for noise and distractions and, if you do have a 'proper' drink, the possibility that it will cloud your thinking or judgement. I like pubs, but make sure that I already know people well before I use one for any sort of meeting.

When to have a one-to-one

To a degree, the date and time to have the meeting need to be decided mutually but just think about it so that you both get the most out of it.

Straight after a morning networking meeting is an ideal time to have a one-to-one. You can most likely stay in the same venue you used for the meeting and you won't yet have any of the distractions that come after you've started your working day.

The other benefit of booking the one-to-one straight after the networking meeting is that you don't have to allow a particular amount of time and don't have to let the one-to-one go on longer than is necessary.

Avoid booking lunch meetings or booking out large periods of time to see people (unless, of course, you're 100 per cent sure that you want to spend two hours or so with them and the two of you are a good fit).

The perils of forgetting to ask the right questions

About five years ago, I was asked for a one-to-one by a new visitor to my local networking group.

This person spent ten whole minutes telling me all about the software she was selling. This software would streamline all of the employee processes in my company. It would deal with new employees and make sure that they received every piece of statutory and company paperwork, would add them into the payroll system and electronically put a tick in place when we'd received the P45 from their previous employer.

When an employee left, this revolutionary piece of programming would calculate any holiday we owed, generate a final payslip and P45 and send a final letter to them.

Along the way, this thing was connected to the Internet and would make absolutely sure that our company was kept up to date with new employee legislation, alerting us if we ever needed to change our employee Terms and Conditions of Employment or any other relevant paperwork.

This speech was delivered with all the benefits highlighted like a true salesperson and, seemingly, not one pause for breath.

Immediately after she finished speaking, she delivered the killer question, 'So Stephen [she got my name wrong], how many employees do you have?'

Can you guess where this story is going?

At the time I was a sole trader. My business comprised me, a Blackberry and a laptop. So I was useless to her. What a waste of her time!

But say she had, instead of broadcasting at me, asked me a few choice questions. She might have found out that several of my clients were human resources consultants, specialising in working with clients with many employees. These referrals would have been ideal for her. But she never gave me the chance to get a word in edgeways before deciding that I was far too small a business for her to bother with anymore.

Interestingly, and hardly surprisingly, I never saw her at a networking event again.

So ask questions. Find out about the person you're talking to.

I once agreed to a lunch with someone, set up by another networking colleague. Before we'd finished the starter, we found that we just didn't hit it off and had both had a different understanding of the premise of our meeting. We had to sit there in a sort of blind date purgatory for the duration of the other two courses, pretending that the meeting was going somewhere when we both knew that it wasn't.

It was a waste of our time and two of the most uncomfortable hours I have ever spent in business.

If you're self-employed, you're not getting an hourly rate to sit and chat to people. If a one-to-one isn't working, be prepared and brave enough to move onto something that is.

Asking open questions

If you want to help a conversation pick up pace, and help the person you're talking with open up and tell you about themselves and their business, you can do so using 'open' questions.

To explain open questions, it makes sense to first explain what a closed question looks like.

A closed question results in the answer 'yes' or 'no'. So if you ask someone, 'Did it take you long to get here?', the conversation may quickly close down. Equally, if you ask 'Have you been to this event before?' you may get a simple 'No'; which leaves you having to resurrect the conversation again.

An open question, on the other hand, helps the conversation to move forward and flow and, if you're meeting someone for the first time, or having a one-to-one with them, can really help you to establish rapport.

Open questions tend to start with 'wh' – such as 'who', 'what', 'why', 'when' and 'where'. Note, however, that 'how' is also often used in open questions.

For example, instead of asking 'Have you been here before?', you can ask 'When were you last at this event?'

Instead of asking 'Do you know anyone else here?', you can instead ask 'Who else do you know who attends this event?'

Every time you ask an open question, it gives you somewhere else to go; for example:

'Do you know anyone else here?'

'Yes.'

'Who else do you know here?'

'I know Jane Smith over there.'

'Oh, how do you know Jane?'

'She supplies us with office stationery.'

'Oh, that's good to know. What's their service like?'

In this way, the conversation can develop.

In the context of the one-to-one, using open questions gives you the opportunity to let the other person expand on telling you about their business and who they are.

Do you know that old adage in sales that people like nothing more than talking about themselves? Asking the 'right' open questions can give you a real insight into who they are.

Here are a few belters that help you to quickly get to know more about your contact:

- ✔ 'So why did you go into business for yourself?'
- ✔ 'Which bits of your work do you really love doing?'
- ✔ 'What does your ideal client look like?'
- ✔ 'What has been your biggest success to date?'
- ✔ 'Who is your best client?'
- ✔ 'What sort of referrals do you like to get?'
- ✔ 'What sort of referrals aren't worth your while?'
- ✔ 'What's the biggest challenge facing your business today?'

Imagine a situation whereby a few days after your one-to-one you're able to pick up the phone and say, 'Phil, you know you told me that your biggest challenge right now was getting in front of the right prospects/getting your bills paid/finding a reliable supplier/imminent zombie attack (delete as appropriate)? Well, I've just met someone who could potentially help; shall I ask him to call you?'

Imagine phoning a few days after your one-to-one and saying, 'Phil, I've been thinking about what you said and reckon my business may be able to help; have you got 20 minutes for a coffee so I can explain?'

If you've already tried to sell during the one-to-one, you won't have that opportunity. If you've found out about the other guy and now are honestly offering a solution, you've increased your chances of success many, many times.

Are you listening or waiting for your turn to speak?

I promised so many of my networking contacts that I'd include the old advice 'You have two ears and one mouth; use them in that proportion', because so many people in networking forget the advice and just talk.

But it goes deeper than that. There's listening and there's *really* listening.

Many people aren't really listening a lot of the time. Many people are listening for the little silence that gives them the cue to start speaking. Many people are listening for you to say something that gives them an excuse to jump in with their bit.

Train yourself to listen. Listen to someone else bearing in mind that you might have to repeat what they've told you later. Listen in the spirit that if you had to sit a test about how well you knew the other person you'd get a respectable score.

Making notes to follow up with

Do make notes about each one-to-one or meeting you have with other networking colleagues.

Download your memory into a paper-based or electronic system. Evernote is good, but the thing is to use a system that helps you to find stuff easily in the future.

Like most people, you won't remember everyone's name but a decent system enables you to search for the guy or gal that does 'ethical web hosting', or the person you met in such-and-such hotel or the florist who was really into The Stranglers. That sort of system makes a huge difference to how you're able to use your network in the future and how easy you find it to pass referrals and recommendations along.

Think of a turbo-charged Rolodex on amphetamines. That's the sort of system I have.

Taking notes like a pro

After you've met someone at a networking meeting, make some quick notes. You'll meet lots of other people and may not remember everything at the end of the meeting.

Take a notebook or use an app such as Evernote to take notes. That way you have more space than scribbling on a business card (and, in some cultures, it's considered extremely disrespectful to deface someone's business card. Even if it isn't culturally sensitive, the person you're speaking to might have just set up their business and spent a lot of cash on business cards. Watching you scribble on one might leave the wrong impression).

Here are three things to record:

- ✓ **Memory hooks about their business.** Make a note of anything that isn't on the card that might help you remember a little more about them when you're back home. For example, 'specialises in pensions' when the card just tells you 'financial adviser', 'expert in e-commerce sites' for a web developer or 'supplies the Duchy of Cornwall' for a mobile phone specialist.

- ✓ **Any personal details to help you remember them.** Examples might be 'went to St Gregory's school about 5 years after me', 'rugby coach at the weekends' or 'massive rock fan; planning to go to Sonisphere this year'. This stuff gives you a hook the next time you speak or follow up.

- ✓ **What you said you'd do next.** The easiest way to not do something is to not make a note of it. If you said 'I'll call you next week', write it down and then get it into your diary system as soon as you get back. If you didn't commit to doing anything, still make a note to follow up at some point, even just out of courtesy.

Knowing What to Do After the Meeting

After you've had your one-to-one, follow up and quickly to thank the other person for their time.

For example, you could send them a tweet:

- ✔ 'Thanks @pointandstare for coffee today; really glad to hear that another old punk is out there.'

- ✔ 'Lovely to meet you @DebbieHuxton – some really inspiring advice you gave me.'

Or email them with a brief note and mention what you liked about the meeting.

If you both felt the potential for something else to happen, get on it now. Take the next step, whether that's another meeting, a phone call or a potential referral for them. Seize the energy and the momentum that comes when something's new and move forward before you talk yourself out of it.

Chapter 10

Breezing Through the Ten-Minute Speaker Slot

⬤ ⬤

In This Chapter

▶ Understanding why you want to volunteer to be the guest speaker

▶ Identifying the best presentations and crafting one for yourself

▶ Recognising what *not* to do – even if you think it's right

⬤ ⬤

*T*hey say that talk is cheap, but actually, the opportunity to demonstrate your expertise and your passion to a select and supportive audience is priceless.

Handled correctly, the opportunity to speak in front of your networking group is potentially the biggest opportunity that networking offers – not least because many members choose to avoid it.

In this chapter, you set up a strategy for turning yourself into one of the sought-after speakers with a reputation for delivering engaging, enjoyable and educational presentations.

Recognising the Opportunity

When I first started going networking, as a fresh-faced 30-something with no business experience (as opposed to the weathered 40-something with many experiences best described as 'character forming' who's currently writing this chapter), I noticed that the groups had speakers at each event.

At the end of each event, an interesting mixture of persuasion, begging and blackmail took place to try to get someone to fill the next speaker slot. Nobody seemed to want to do it; those who did were reluctant and, as a result, we often got the same guy week after week.

My initial impressions were that this public moment was something to be dreaded and avoided, that blaming shyness and lack of presentation skills was the way forward and a reputation for not wanting to speak in public was to be cultivated, to save having to politely decline every week.

Interestingly, at the same time I admired and was somewhat in awe of the people who did step up to the mark. These people were obviously heavyweights in the business arena; people of such standing and experience that they could stand up and educate and illuminate the rest of us. Truly, these people were to be emulated in business.

It took me far too long to realise that a simple, if at the time terrifying, way to emulate these entrepreneurial giants was to do exactly what they were doing and be the speaker. I realised that I didn't have to be perfect on my first attempt; that, actually, these guys and gals most likely had built up to their seemingly effortless performances over time.

Something else I noticed was that I never remembered every single 40-second introduction, no matter how large or small the networking group was. I was always far too busy concentrating on (a) remembering the individuals I wanted to have a one-to-one with and (b) mentally rehearsing my own 40 seconds. But I did always remember the speaker; no matter what they spoke about or how well they did it, they always left an impression and I was always particularly impressed that they'd stood up to do it, while equally grateful that they'd saved me from having to do so.

Once I realised the opportunity that being the speaker represented, I saw that it gave me the chance to accelerate my networking, and therefore my business profile, quickly and with little investment.

The ten-minute presentation is too big an opportunity not to take advantage of. Business Network International (BNI) calls it the 'Launchpad' presentation; we at 4Networking call it the 4Sight. Other organisations use different descriptions but still do it. And enjoy it.

Reaping the benefits

Modern business networking gives modern business people
an opportunity that would have been prohibitively expensive
for those from previous generations.

Had you set up a business 20 years ago and wanted to go
around the country speaking on your specialist subject in
front of other business people, your potential target market,
it would have been difficult to organise.

You'd have had to:

- Find a venue
- Find someone locally to promote your presentation
- Advertise the event locally
- Give something away so that people were willing to come
  along
- Pay for a venue and refreshments

Today you can just ask your networking organisation to find
vacant speaker slots and volunteer yourself to fill them – with
an almost guaranteed audience of business people to sit and
listen to you.

Being the speaker enables you to:

- Build your public speaking confidence and ability in a
  supportive environment
- Demonstrate your expertise in your field
- Show your passion about your chosen profession or
  business
- Give real value to your fellow networkers
- Establish yourself as an expert
- Increase your 'stock value' (see the next section) among
  your crowd
- Develop your own knowledge of your subject by
  researching and understanding material outside of your
  own experience
- Take on more speaking opportunities if you want them

Understanding stock value

I talk sometimes about 'stock value' and should explain what I mean, as sometimes stock value can be misinterpreted.

Imagine a combination of your profile, your reputation and the number of people in your networking circles willing to recommend you and support your business. When you first start out, if you expressed all of those things as a stock value, that value would be low. No matter how good you are at what you do, if nobody knows about it, then it isn't yet a business. The more networking you do, the more you build your crowd and your advocates, and the more you refine and improve your business, the higher your stock value climbs. Sometimes you get a setback, like a bad client, or you have to step away from networking for a while and your stock value shrinks as you lose close contacts and advocates. Sometimes you get a bit of luck, such as a major client, and your stock value increases.

Several companies can measure people's stock value online in various ways, but you're likely to be the better judge if you're truly honest with yourself. Where do you think your value is right now? If I set a scale of 1 to 100, where would you mark yourself? What can you do to improve it right now? Do it.

Planning and Preparing

If you've been invited to, or have volunteered to, present at your networking group for the first time, start planning your presentation at least ten days before the event.

Planning it at 10:00 p.m. the night before once you've got the kids off to bed and filled the dishwasher really isn't the way forward here. Not only will you be stressed but you'll have no time to rework your content if what was in your head turns out to be only two minutes' worth of presentation. (I've seen that happen several times – painfully embarrassing for both the presenter and audience.)

Give yourself time to get all of your stress out of the way before the day you present it. Give yourself time to rehearse it and get super-confident with the material.

Looking at Different Networks, Different Opportunities, Different Approaches

Broadly speaking, you find two types of speaking opportunity at networking events. Each has its own pros and cons and each requires a different approach. Despite the differing approaches, however, these two speaking opportunities use similar strategies and presentation methods.

Firstly, some organisations allow you to deliver a presentation specifically on your business. The purpose of this presentation is to enable you to, supposedly, educate other members about your business and the type of referrals you're looking for. Members of the networking group can then actively seek referrals for you from within their contacts. Think of it as a ten-minute sales pitch with a captive audience.

Secondly, some organisations allow you to present as long as it *isn't* a sales pitch. The purpose of this presentation is summed up in the old adage 'people buy people'. This approach enables you to build a close relationship with your audience through an engaging presentation, which may be about a business subject, or a part of your life, or another interest you're passionate about. Some of the best presentations I've seen have been about something that the presenter is interested in and how that links to their business and their passion for their business.

Neither style of presentation is right or wrong, although I personally prefer listening to the latter, and each takes some thought to get right.

Using ten minutes to talk about your business

Anyone can talk about their business for ten minutes. If you love what you do, if you're truly passionate about what you do, then of course you can wax lyrical about it.

Incidentally, if you're not passionate about your business, or don't bore everyone silly with how excited you are about waking up every morning and going to work, and you can't imagine talking about it for ten minutes, then find the thing you *are* incredibly passionate about and work out how you turn that into a business instead.

That said, you know the guy who only ever talks about his business and never lets you get a word in edgeways? Yes, that guy. The guy whose conversation makes you feel as though you're looking at someone else's holiday photos? Photos that are incredibly interesting to them and them only.

You need to make sure that you're not that guy when you do your presentation about your business. You need to work out what's going to keep people interested for ten minutes and stop them drifting off and thinking about that phone call they have to make at 10:00 a.m. and whether Steve is still off sick today.

Asking, 'So what?'

Before planning your ten-minute presentation in any detail, consider two words: 'So what?'

Start by getting out a blank piece of paper and writing down what you do. Make as many individual lines of text as possible. If you're like most people in the world (although most people in the world haven't yet bought this book and really should), you start with something like:

> We provide insurance to small businesses.

or

> Our company was established ten years ago and we are Oxford's leading employment law solicitors.

or

> I create brand identities and graphic designs for all sorts of businesses.

When you've written down what you think you do, I want you to write those two words next to each line.

SO WHAT?

And then answer the question.

After you've answered it, write SO WHAT? next to that line again. And then keep going. For example:

> We provide insurance to small businesses. SO WHAT?
>
> So that each business has the appropriate insurance. SO WHAT?
>
> So that you know that your business has the right insurance. SO WHAT?
>
> So that your business is protected from litigation and unforeseen challenges. SO WHAT?
>
> So that your business can keep going even if the worst happens. SO WHAT?
>
> So that you as a business owner can sleep at night knowing that even if the worst happened your business would be protected, you'd be able to carry on paying your mortgage and your children's school fees and your income would hardly be affected.

Ah. You've got it!

You see most people focus on what they *do* rather than the effect it has. Most people can tell you the ins and outs of what their business does, but the question that the listener wants answered is, of course, 'What's in it for me?' So, if I buy whatever you're selling, what difference does that make to my life?

Often the answer to that question, when selling business to business, is along the lines of:

- ✔ Does it make me more money?
- ✔ Does it save me money and therefore make me more profitable?
- ✔ Does it make my life easier, save me time and therefore make me more profitable?
- ✔ Does it make it easier for customers to buy from me and therefore make me more sales?
- ✔ Does it give clients more confidence in buying from me and therefore make me more sales?
- ✔ Does it remove a problem or worry, even if I didn't know I had that problem or worry in the first place?

Spend time thinking about these questions and writing the answers down now. If you find it easier, work with a friend or your business partner to work out what you really do and what real value you bring to your customers or clients. Get this value down before you even think of presenting your business to other people.

Setting out a structure to talk about your business

As with any presentation, or indeed writing a *For Dummies* book, it makes sense to start off with a structure and then base the presentation around that.

A structure makes planning and writing easier and acts as a sensible memory aid when you come to presenting. If you remember the order in which you put the structure together, you're more easily able to remember where you're up to and what comes next than if everything was in a random order.

So, to talk about your business, a suggested structure may be:

1. **Who you are and what it says above the door** (how most people would describe your business; for example, accountant or surveyor or financial adviser).

2. **Why you're qualified to do this job and what journey got you to where you are now** (you worked for a large company or organisation for 20 years and decided you could offer better value by going it alone).

3. **What you do.** Think about 'So what?' above. Give two or three examples of what you do that actually mean something to the other people in the room.

4. **Case study.** Make it real. Talk about an actual client you've worked with who fits the profile of the networking members in the room. Explain what you did, why it added value and what the client said about you afterwards.

5. **Who you want to work with and why.** In a referral organisation, explain specifically who you want to work with and why you believe you can help them. Be specific and, above all, be honest.

6. **Explain where people can find out more information and the best ways to contact you to do business with you or pass you a referral.**

Using ten minutes not to talk about your business

Arguably, *not* talking about your business can be more difficult than talking about it. Sometimes people even ask me whether talking about something else is pointless – if they're at a networking event, they want to promote their business.

By finding a way of not talking about your business, but engaging with the audience and demonstrating your expertise, your passion or just a side of you outside the business world, you can quickly fast-forward relationships and develop your reputation and profile.

The following sections look at several different types of presentation that don't involve telling people why they should use you.

Giving stuff away for free

Well, maybe not 'stuff' as such, but knowledge.

A worthwhile ten-minute presentation is one where you give your audience information that, if they take it away and use it, can save them money or enable them to do something they would otherwise need to pay you for.

For example, if you specialise in search engine optimisation, you may spend your ten minutes telling people how to use blogging and article submission to boost their website's visibility on Google. Plus you might give people ten sites they can submit articles to for free.

If you're a copywriter, you might explain to people how to lay out their web pages to make them readable and compelling to humans as well as to Google. If you're a builder, you may tell people what steps they can take to prevent damage to their property and save potential repair bills in future.

This move is really counter-intuitive – and has proved spectacularly successful for many people who practise it.

But why would you give your knowledge away for free? Surely you're doing yourself out of business?

Actually no, you're creating more business.

By giving away your knowledge and expertise for free, you can quickly establish yourself as an expert in your field. By explaining how you do what you do, you show yourself to be open and transparent.

You also give your audience massive value in that ten minutes, with information that they can take away and use if they wish to. At the same time, you get your audience thinking about improving their search engine optimisation, or making the words on their website better, or fixing up those little jobs around the home.

Those people who'd usually try to do it for themselves will still do so. Hopefully, you've helped them to do it better than they would have done in the first place and, in future, you now have a better chance that they'll call you in as they've seen how skilled you are.

But most people stick to what they're good at and leave the experts to do what they're good at. You've just established yourself as that expert.

Plus (and this point is a major benefit in networking), people in the room now know that you're an expert. When they come across a contact who needs what you supply, they find it much easier to refer or recommend you as, even if they haven't used your services, you've impressed them with your knowledge.

Get a blank piece of paper. What knowledge or tips can you give your audience that you would feel confident talking about and would show them just how much you know?

Structure the presentation along these lines:

1. **Introduce yourself.**
2. **Tell them what you're going to talk about.**
3. **Explain why you're qualified to talk about it.**
4. **Give them your tips or knowledge.**
5. **Summarise.**

Talking about your passion

What led you to your current business? What specifically in your life helped you to choose this path?

How about explaining to people why you deeply love and care about what you do and plot a path for them so that they can see how you have your business ingrained in your DNA.

One of the most memorable presentations that I've ever seen was delivered by a bookkeeper. I don't wish to offend any bookkeepers out there but from the outside it looks like a pretty dry subject, adding up receipts and the like. I consider myself to be a 'creative', which means I don't 'get' how someone can be interested in those numbers. Or at least I didn't until I saw this presentation.

The bookkeeper explained about her life-long love of travel. How throughout her childhood and into her adult life she'd always enjoyed holidays and, to a large extent, enjoyed the journey just as much as the destination. She told us about a few of her more memorable trips in an engaging and amusing way.

Then she explained that she adores looking at the books and figures for a business as these books give away the journey that business has taken. Within the numbers, she explained, you can see the stop off points along the way. You can see where the business took a wrong turn, when it got stuck in traffic and when it had a clear run and could accelerate for a while.

So, every time she was working with a company she was enjoying the journey with them. She got to see that journey and that was where her passion came from.

It was tangible, it made sense to everyone in the room and a dry subject was covered without actually being covered.

What truly turns you on about your business? I know that I've said this elsewhere in the book but if the answer is 'nothing really', please go and find the thing that does excite you and see whether you can make a business out of that instead. Then read this book again when you're truly loving life.

Is it the journey in the numbers? Do you love looking at a building and being able to see what's solid and what needs fixing? Can you look at a house and immediately see how the owners can extend and improve it? Does the beauty of language excite you, so you want to help every business describe and explain itself better?

Write down a list of what really excites you about your business and work out a way of weaving that into a presentation.

Thinking about your journey

What have you discovered along the way? What skills and expertise did you pick up in a previous career that you've brought to your current role or business?

My journey is relevant to where I am and what I'm doing now. A lot of what I was doing for the almost 20 years before getting involved in business networking helped me to build the skills and knowledge that I've been able to transfer to my current field.

While what you used to do might not feel relevant now, I bet that you can find aspects that you can directly trace back.

Within my own network are the following:

- ✔ The ex-professional dancer who learned about preparation and how no substitute exists for practice and rehearsal. She now builds teams in an international business.

- ✔ The ex-airline cabin crew member who discovered how to stay calm in a crisis and now applies that to her work as a human resources consultant. Nothing is ever going to be as stressful as a plane's engine catching fire and having to calm down hysterical passengers.

- ✔ The ex-military officer who now coaches management teams. He has lots of experience in how to make sure that tasks are delegated properly and that people are given concise and clear instructions.

Write down a list of your skills. Make a note of what you've found out along the way that can help the people around you understand where you came from and why you run your business as you do.

Explaining your passions outside work

You can reap benefits from talking to people about what else you do outside of your work. One of the most obvious benefits is that it makes you human.

People can easily label someone based on what they do, but the extra bits, the social habits and quirky side of someone's nature, that's what's memorable. You might be an accountant and yet, outside work, sing in a punk rock band. You might be a garden designer who loves genealogy.

As well as proving that you're human and not just the 'at work' version of yourself that people are used to seeing, you've also just given everyone else in your networking group another way to remember you.

On their mental picture of you, they now don't just have 'accountant' but they can also mentally affix the label 'punk rock singer'.

Don't forget that you want to be memorable when someone comes across the person who needs a new accountant, or whatever service you provide. Giving someone extra memory labels for you helps them bring you to the front of their mind when you most need them to be able to.

You've also given people another topic of conversation with you and potentially something in common with other people in the room. Those who don't share the same interest as you will be interested; those who do will feel a connection.

Another, more subtle benefit, is that we find it easier to talk about subjects we're comfortable with. If you're a collector of vintage motorbikes, you most likely know that subject so well that you can speak with ease. Your passion and confidence on your subject are obvious and it helps get you used to speaking in front of an audience.

Be careful to make your presentation interesting and engaging. Make sure that you put anecdotes in there that are funny to everyone.

Presenting the big message

Do you have an over-riding message that you want to get across in your presentation? Did you learn one specific lesson from your background or part of your journey? Have you been taught a lesson along the way or has your background reinforced some knowledge? Do you want to make sure that your audience learns from your experience?

Sometimes you need to start at the end and work backwards. If you want to deliver a message or series of messages, you need to make sure that every aspect of your presentation leads towards that. Write down the message first. Make it concise and powerful by stripping out every unnecessary word and paring it down to a basic point that people can easily remember and take away with them.

 If you want people to quote your messages and talk about your presentation, make sure that your soundbites are shorter than 120 characters or so. That enables people to tweet what you've said and include your name, spreading the popularity of your presentation.

Check the anecdotes that you're using. Do they reinforce your message or are they just there for the sake of it?

If you explain your anecdotes to someone else, does that other person 'get' why they reinforce a particular piece of wisdom? Think of Aesop's fables; we all 'got' the story of the tortoise and the hare. We understood from an early age the

When nerves run away with you

My nerves occasionally used to interrupt my presentations. They don't do so anymore but only because I've discovered the following techniques to use if I feel myself becoming nervous.

If it happens to you – your mouth becomes dry or your mind goes blank – you can easily get back on track.

Firstly, stop talking. Take a second to get your breath back. Pick up the glass of water and spend ten seconds bringing it slowly to your mouth and taking enough of a sip to stop your mouth being dry. Breathe slowly as you bring it up to your mouth and, once you've sipped, as you slowly place it back on the table. Concentrate on the glass and your breathing.

Then, pick up your longhand notes, find where you were in the presentation and start reading aloud. You can read out loud for as long as you need to but it really won't take long before your mind wakes up again and you're back on track.

You'll be the only person who's noticed your nerves. Everyone else in the room will just presume you needed a drink and your preparation means that you have everything to hand to deal with it.

message that that story was telling, both the basic story and the underlying message too. Are your anecdotes almost as simple? If not, they need to be.

Make sure that you end your presentation by spelling out the message itself, succinctly and clearly.

Structuring Your Presentation

Remember that every presentation needs to have a beginning, a middle and an end.

More than that, for your ten-minute presentation to make sense to the audience, you need to set people's expectations, deliver what you planned to deliver and then summarise.

The tried-and-tested format for a great presentation is the following:

1. **Tell them what you're about to tell them.**
2. **Tell them.**
3. **Tell them what you've just told them.**

Or to put it another way:

1. **Introduce yourself and briefly outline the point of your presentation.**
2. **Deliver the main body of the presentation.**
3. **Summarise the main learning point and close.**

If you have ten minutes, then allow around one minute for the introduction, six minutes for the main body and one further minute for your close.

Then you still have two minutes to answer questions.

Questions and answers

You need to allow time at the end for questions from the audience.

This time enables you to engage further with the audience, allows them to ask for clarification if there was anything they didn't understand and allows you to correct any misunderstandings.

The connection and conversation you can build is priceless and really allows you to further demonstrate your expertise.

No matter what your presentation is about, remember to smile all the way through and let your audience see that you're enjoying talking to them.

The exception to the previous tip is when your subject is sad or deadly serious, but I'm sure that you guessed this anyway!

Checking your timings

Rehearse your presentation just as you would any other and, moreover, rehearse with a clock in front of you.

When you've crafted a fabulous presentation, that you know will wow your audience and leave them falling over themselves to talk further with you, you really don't want to have to rush the end because the group leader has just given you the universal 'wind it up' hand signal.

Write the presentation out in full and get used to reading it out loud. Read it in your normal tone and speed of speech and time yourself. If you realise you've gone over time, look at the content again and see what you can lose. Then read it out loud again and time it. Repeat the process until you get it right and then read it out loud at least once a day before you have to present it.

Coping when the day comes

When the day comes, have two versions of your presentation printed out and with you. Have one version with the major headings in a large font that you can easily see if they're on the table in front of you, and another with the whole thing typed out longhand in case you need to read out loud.

Print two copies of each version. Place one in your pocket or bag and leave one on the passenger seat of the car. This idea sounds mad but if you're at all nervous it will help you to know that you cannot lose your notes. Even if they suddenly do that thing which stuff you need tends to do – disappear into that secret compartment in your bag just at the point at which you need it – you know that you've got another copy a few steps away in the car.

If a break in proceedings is being held before you're due to present, go to the toilet. If you're American, go to the bathroom instead. Do what people do in the toilet. Go for a wee. I know you think you can last until the end of the presentation but get it out of the way now so that it doesn't become suddenly urgent, particularly if you're drinking water as you speak.

After you're done (and have washed your hands), take a look in the mirror. Much better you discover now, while you still have time to do something about it, that your zip is undone, your bra strap is showing or you've got fried egg in your beard, rather than immediately after the presentation in the full knowledge that you stood up for ten minutes looking like that.

Before you stand up to speak, make sure that you find somewhere you can put your notes within sight of where you're standing. You've rehearsed and memorised the presentation so successfully that you really only need the major headings but you have the safety net of the full text just in case.

Make sure that you have a small glass of water within reach. You may want to sip it during the presentation and will definitely want to afterwards.

Place a small clock, watch or the clock of your mobile phone where you can see it and check timings without the audience being aware that you're doing so. If a wall clock is in the room within your eye-line, great. Otherwise, take off your watch and place it in front of you by your notes. Being aware of the timings yourself reassures you that you're on track throughout. Time passes differently when you're presenting in front of people. It just does.

If you're going to use the clock on your mobile phone as your timer, turn your phone to Airplane Mode and set it so that the screen doesn't switch off for at least the length of your presentation. The last thing you want to happen is for the phone number of Mr Angry Client Who You Forgot To Call Back Yesterday to suddenly appear on the screen as you're presenting and put you off. The second last thing you want is for the screen to go blank at four minutes leaving you no idea where you're up to for the rest of the presentation.

When it's time to present, take a deep breath, stand up and blow their socks off.

Death by PowerPoint

I've seen few ten-minute presentations that were enhanced by PowerPoint slides.

With only ten minutes to fill, I strongly recommend against using PowerPoint or similar for several reasons.

Firstly, and most importantly, you're giving yourself something else to stress about. Including technology when you only have ten minutes to fill and probably only have two or three minutes to set up feels like a recipe for disaster to me.

Are any of you old enough to remember *Tomorrow's World*? The BBC television programme that featured upcoming technology and which convinced us in the 1970s that, by the year 2000, our lives would be transformed by machines doing all the work, leaving us to seek leisure activities to fill our time?

The other thing which *Tomorrow's World* showed us, as it used to be broadcast live, is that technology works fine right up to the point when it needs to and you have an audience. At that exact moment it develops an error, or just shuts down completely. Then, just when you no longer need it, it chooses to rise like a phoenix from the ashes and magically start working again.

Secondly, for ten minutes you want your audience to have as few distractions as possible. You've a limited time to get your message across and, if they're trying to read your slides as well as listen to your voice, they may be distracted.

They may also be distracted when a Skype message appears on the screen, or Windows decides now is exactly the right time to perform an update.

Thirdly, I've seen so few PowerPoint slides that add something to the presentation. You may be a PowerPoint expert, but most people aren't. Be honest with yourself about that.

Chapter 11

Following Up

. . . .

In This Chapter

▶ Building a system to ensure that you follow up every time

▶ Selling without selling – reminding people who you are without being pushy

▶ Tools to make following up so much simpler

. . . .

*F*ollowing up after a business networking event creates momentum and takes the relationship with your contact forward, potentially to the stage where you actually talk business. It reminds each contact of your existence outside the networking meeting and, because so few people remember to follow up, immediately sets you apart from everyone else.

In this chapter, I explain how to follow up, when to follow up and who to follow up. You build a strategy that, if you follow it, ensures that at the very least you have a stream of enquiries. This strategy also builds you a profile and a gang of advocates who can recommend and refer you.

Following Up to Win

This follow up, dear reader, is where it often goes wrong – for other people of course, not you, because you've taken the time to buy and read this book.

For other people, it goes wrong. People who spend hours perfecting their introduction, people who invest in leaflets explaining what they do, people who put a banner up at meetings with their details and website address in full view, people who handle their one-to-ones perfectly; people who then do nothing after the meeting to keep in touch.

You see, the networking extends far beyond the networking event you've just left. The networking event really is just the start of the process. The networking event is your first intro-duction. What you do afterwards is what makes the difference to whether all of this work starts to turn into business for you. How you conduct yourself after the meeting, as much as during the meeting, builds your reputation and profile out there. You'll find it, frankly, more important to get things right after the meeting than during the meeting.

Think on the following: you don't remember every conversa-tion you had at your networking meetings last week, and the meetings you went to last month are a complete blur. Even that guy who really impressed you – you remember, *that* guy – if I pressed you now, you wouldn't remember his website address or contact details.

And everyone else?

They don't remember you.

You've invested all this time and money into networking and the very people you're trying to impress have got caught up with their own stuff, their own businesses, their own life.

This chapter makes sure that they do remember you.

Ouch! Dealing with Your Piles

That guy who you met at a networking event last month, the one who was really interested in your services? You remem-ber? He said he was thinking about using someone who did what you do, probably not this month because he's just fin-ishing off an important project, but next month when that's sorted he definitely wants to do something about it.

What did you do with his business card? And the business cards of all the other people you met recently at networking events?

Can I make a guess? Are they in a pile on your desk? Or do you have a special little box to keep them in? Or do they go into the third drawer down, along with the posh paper and posh envelopes you're going to use to send personal letters to people – when you get round to it?

See, most people who go networking eventually develop a problem with piles. Nope, it isn't all the fried food, or the unnaturally early mornings upsetting their natural rhythm. These piles are the piles of business cards that you keep meaning to do something with and then don't.

Making the most of business cards

You spent money on your business cards (I hope). You employed a graphic designer to make them look fabulous, you employed a printer to get the feel of them right and you, proudly when you first started your business, handed them out to people at networking events.

When I was employed, the business card was an incredibly important part of me. Far too important, I realised later. The business card gave me an identity. I wasn't 'just' Stefan Thomas. I was Stefan Thomas – Assistant Branch Manager, or Stefan Thomas – General Manager. Maybe it's a male thing and maybe it's an English male thing, but my cards helped define me, and I still have every card from every job I've ever had stashed somewhere in my house.

When I became self-employed, I remember being incredibly proud of my first set of cards for my new 'business' (which was more a hobby at the time – I spent a lot of time on it but didn't seem to make any money – but I had business cards so I could call it a business).

Culturally we (the English) take our business cards nowhere near as seriously as other cultures and nations do. But think about all the effort that someone has taken to make their business card, just for you to go and put it in a pile, which you'll get round to doing something about one day.

 If your business cards have words on the back to the effect of 'Supplied free by XXX. Get your free cards here', please, please, please dump them and spend a tiny bit of money on decent cards. The impression you're giving is that you're not prepared to invest in your own business. And if you're not, why should I? If you know a printer in your preferred networking group, please go and talk to them.

Use both sides of your business card. Put something on the back as well as the front and use up all the real estate you have. Some people even have a little space for notes or an appointment date on the back of the card, which I think is quite neat. But use both sides.

The demise of the business card has long been predicted. Nowadays you can find apps for your smart phone that easily send contact details between one phone and another. In fact, that's been possible for at least ten years now. Now that we all have our contacts stored on our smart phones, now that we have Microsoft Outlook or Google Contacts, now that everyone is on LinkedIn or Facebook anyway, why do we need little bits of card with our contact details printed on one side?

The business card resolutely remains one of the mainstays for anyone in business of any sort. If you're asked for a business card at an event and you don't have one, you feel left out. If you ask someone else for a card and they don't have one, you may wonder why not.

Instead of just putting them into a pile, why not do something with them?

The simplest and least technological thing to do with a business card is to make notes on the card itself at the meeting. However, and importantly, I'm writing this book for the UK market; in some cultures, defacing someone's business card can be hugely offensive.

When you get the annotated card home, enter the details into a system that suits you. The following sections look at how you might do that.

Smart phone technology

These days, however, you don't necessarily need a dedicated business-card scanner. Many smartphones do the job for you, with the added benefit that you're likely to have them with you at a networking meeting, when you actually need them.

Using the inbuilt camera on your smart phone, you can find apps, typically free, that can take a photo of a business card, then read the information on it and prepare the data ready to go into whichever format you want it to.

I'm a devotee of Evernote and personally use Evernote Hello as my business-card scanner. At the end of any one-to-one meeting, I can quickly take a photo of the business card and have the information entered instantly into Evernote and my iPhone contacts. It can even go off and find the person on LinkedIn and give me the option of connecting with them there and then.

The added advantage is that I can make notes about the person without defacing their card, plus enter a follow-up action and Evernote will give me a reminder to do so.

LinkedIn actually has its own system (CardMunch) that does broadly the same – turning the business card into a contact entry and allowing you to connect on LinkedIn at the same time.

You can also find many other card scanners in the App Store, Google Play Store (and the Windows and Blackberry equivalents, too).

As with any technology, what you're comfortable using is more important than what's popular.

Business card scanners

Many devices on the market can scan business cards in for you, saving you the trouble of entering the information into a system manually. For less than £100, you can buy something that plugs into the USB port of your laptop or computer and, within seconds, has electronically read every card you collected and turned the information into a contact record.

The information is then sent straight to Outlook, Act! or most other contact and customer relationship management (CRM) systems.

Technology never ceases to amaze me. How can a little machine read a card and know which bit is the person's name and which is the company name? What an age we live in!

I've used these devices in the past and they're typically very accurate and useful. If you prefer to do stuff on your laptop rather than your smart phone, these devices really are a good answer.

Using CRM systems

CRM stands for 'Contact Relationship Management' and, put simply, is a system that enables you to not only store the details of your contacts, but also build some automation into how and when you communicate with those contacts.

The market seems to have grown exponentially in recent years and many, many systems are on the market. I list a few of the more popular options here but you probably have your own preference and may even find someone in your networking circles who specialises in CRM.

Over and above a simple electronic address book, a decent CRM allows you to make notes about any contact, record a whole load of information about them, which you may find useful in future, schedule things like calls and to-dos so you don't forget and even put meetings in your diary when you agree them.

I thoroughly recommend that you invest in some sort of system, though. Even if you prefer a paper-based system to one of the many 'whizzy' shiny electronic ones out there, find a system that suits you and stick to it.

Some of the electronic, and less techy systems, available out there include:

- ✔ **The Filofax:** That symbol of yuppie status from the 1980s (do they even say 'yuppie' anymore?). Many people still swear by it and enjoy the simplicity of pencil and paper.

- ✔ **Microsoft Outlook:** If your background is corporate, you're probably horribly familiar with the email capabilities of Outlook and have probably even stored your contacts in there too. You may even have it set up to synchronise with your phone's address book. Scratch beneath the surface, and Outlook can do loads more, with a highly sophisticated calendar function and even the ability to set Tasks that give you reminders to do them.

- ✔ **Google Calendar/Google Contacts:** I personally use Google Calendar and Google Contacts along with add-ons to make it into a CRM. This software works beautifully for me and you can even find online CRMs that you can subscribe to and that synchronise with Google.

✔ **Act!:** I'm not sure if Act! was the first CRM out there but I was using it in the 1990s and it still remains popular. Act! enables you to set up a sequence of events to happen after you start the sequence off. For example, if you enter the contact today, it reminds you to send an email tomorrow and then put in a phone call in seven days' time. This ability is where the system becomes incredibly powerful and can really add value to what you're doing.

✔ **Contact Maker:** This CRM by CMB Soft is a newer alternative to the more traditional CRMs, with a focus on the basics and getting the simple things right. A traditional and locally installed piece of software, Contact Maker even has functions for, ultimately, invoicing the contact when they've become a client.

✔ **iComplete:** This system has the benefit of being online so can be accessed from wherever users happen to be (so long as they have an Internet connection). You subscribe rather than buy the software, which makes it affordable, and you also find a whole range of things you can do to customise it.

One of the things that I really like about both Contact Maker and iComplete is that the people involved in the development and sales are themselves active networkers. They understand what someone out networking needs from the software.

Evaluating email marketing software

It feels right to talk about email marketing software at this stage, which can be run independently or linked up to many of the proprietary CRM systems. If you're planning to regularly email your contacts, then email marketing software makes it simpler to send many emails at once and also gives you the option to make fancy-looking and personalised emails; the sort that say 'Hi Stefan' at the top.

If you're planning to run email marketing campaigns, you *must* ask your contacts' specific permission before putting their names on a list. Having met someone at a networking event isn't enough – you end up turning people off if you add them to a mailing list without permission. Your message will be lost and they'll send all your future emails to the spam folder.

Following Up Successfully

In the previous sections, I talk about the tools and the principles; now I look at a suggested strategy for following up with your contacts. First, I look at the mechanics, before looking at what to say or write.

If you tell someone during a networking meeting or a one-to-one that you're going to follow up, you have a huge opportunity to disappoint them before you even really get to know them. You're no longer 16; you no longer have to play hard to get. If you tell someone you're going to follow up, then do so. Otherwise, you have broken your first promise to them. If you don't even follow up now, how can they trust you to do anything you've said you're going to do?

Here's a method to get you started:

1. **Have a one-to-one at a networking meeting.**

2. **Collect their card.**

3. **At the meeting or immediately afterwards, record some information about what you discussed and anything else you want to.**

4. **Enter their card details and any other information into your chosen system as soon as possible.**

5. **If you're going to actively use social media, then connect with them on LinkedIn or Twitter or both.**

6. **Email them or send a message on LinkedIn.**

7. **Make that call if you want to meet up again.**

When you connect with people on LinkedIn, don't use their standard 'I'd like to add you to my professional network' message. This kind of message is a complete passion killer. Instead, personalise the message; try something like 'Hi Steve, great to meet you this morning, how about we connect on here too?' or 'Hi Gita, I really was interested in your business, can we connect on here and maybe hook up for a coffee soon?' Just write something that demonstrates that you're not just randomly connecting with people but have actually chosen that person to be a connection.

Thinking about your follow up

What do you want to achieve from this follow up? Are you looking for an appointment to meet up with the person? Or just to stay on their radar for now? Think about the answers to these three questions and that should help you to decide what to do next.

Perhaps you want to get to know more about the other person. Perhaps you've got an inkling that what they have might be really suitable for your business, or vice versa. Or perhaps you honestly think that you might be able to refer people to them, or vice versa.

I hope you finished your one-to-one by asking whether you could call them and set up a coffee sometime. But even if you didn't, you know them now. They are, by definition, a 'warm' lead now that you've talked to them at a networking event.

I'm sure lots and lots of complicated ways exist to achieve these things: ways to approach people; exactly what to say; the perfect timing between sending the follow up email and then calling someone.

And you know what works just as well? Picking up the phone and actually talking to them without an email first.

In a world where emails have taken over, you can stand out if you're brave enough to simply pick up the phone.

If you want a really clever script to get you started, how about the following:

> 'Hi Phil, it's Stef. We met at 4N in Witney this morning. I've been thinking about our one-to-one and wondered if you've got time for a coffee sometime soon?'

But what if you just want to stay on people's radar? Is there any need to waste their time and yours meeting up after the meeting?

These days, social media enables you to keep in touch with people in a professional or informal way (or both) without spending time meeting up. You can explore the relationship first so easily using modern tools.

You can also move faster with social media than if you rely on waiting to have meetings with people. The relationship can be built more quickly and, when and if you do need to meet up with someone, the relationship has already moved from 'warm' to 'friendly'.

Remember the small talk you used to do at the beginning of sales meetings and new relationships? Getting to know people, who they were, what football team they supported (I don't follow football at all, so that was always lost on me), whether they had kids?

You can do all of that now in the bits in-between meetings. Learn to use social media as part of your follow-up strategy. Come to that, if you haven't already learned to use social media, then do that first. This book devotes a whole Part to the subject, plus several excellent *For Dummies* books cover social media in even more detail (search for 'social media' on www.dummies.com to find the right book for you).

Or find the social media guru in your local networking group and spend time with them.

When you want to keep in touch, use social media. If you want to actually talk to someone, use the phone.

Being creative

Over time, I've heard of some truly brilliant ways of following up that people have used when they *really* want to get in front of someone.

The very first thing to do before you follow up with someone is to have a look at their business. Look at the notes you made after the one-to-one, check out their website, blog, LinkedIn profile and Twitter timeline. Try to identify what you have in common.

This stuff is gold dust! In the olden days, you had to get to know people in real life before you knew what you had in common with them. Nowadays, you can be armed with all of that before you next meet at a networking event or follow up one-to-one.

Wish you were here?

A friend of mine, Phil, uses postcards in his follow ups.

Instead of an email or a LinkedIn or Facebook message, he sends a personally addressed postcard with a personally written message.

Sounds a bit quaint and old-fashioned? Consider the following for a second.

During your working day, how many emails do you delete without reading them? Or how many emails do you file away to be read later and never get round to it?

If you got a short punchy postcard through the post – with a message about your business – would you feel more or less inclined to take the sender's call when he phones you?

How about a postcard with a quick message saying 'Just wanted to say I really loved your blog Stef, particularly the article about what to wear' or something along those lines? You're definitely going to take the sender's call when he does phone you. You might even pick up the phone to thank them, or send them a tweet.

Imagine how much easier the first part of some of my follow ups are when I discover, usually from Twitter or Facebook, that the other person likes going to rock or punk gigs, or has children, or likes Swedish crime fiction, or doesn't like football, or loves rugby union, or is a bit bored by Formula 1 these days, or loves marmite, or can't stand celery.

I've over-emphasised that point.

But we live in a world where you can now discover that stuff about people in advance and then keep the conversation going on that basis.

Earlier in this chapter, I said that using the phone in an age of email and social media would get you noticed. Think about other methods that can also help you stand out.

When you're following up, to be effective remember that one size does not fit all.

Reminding People about Your Business

Some people think that selling is somehow a dirty word. But what if, honestly, the services you provide would really suit the person you're talking to? What if you *know* that you can add value to their business, or save them money on something they're already buying, or make something much more efficient for them?

If that's the case, then you're doing them and yourself a disservice if you don't ask them whether you can meet up or spend ten minutes on the phone to give them an idea of what you're thinking.

Blanket selling – selling to everyone – doesn't work in networking any more than it does in real life. Using your one-to-one meetings to get to know someone and then letting them know whether you honestly believe your service would work for them is appropriate and honest.

Asking for business

You can find some excellent books on selling, including, of course, *Selling For Dummies*, co-authored by the clever Ben Kench (Wiley). But a few basics exist that are worth getting across here.

It's okay to ask for business. Apparently, as a nation, the British don't excel at doing so.

Someone once said to me that, having explained your services or products to someone, having shown them your website or brochure, having bought them a coffee, having taken up your time and theirs, isn't it impolite if you don't then ask for the business at the end of the conversation?

If you believe that about your product or service, and you really should, why wouldn't you, at the appropriate time and to the right prospect, ask if they wanted to buy it?

- ✔ 'So shall we go ahead, then, Steve?'
- ✔ 'Shall I get a small order in now so you can trial us?'
- ✔ 'Would you like to join?'

Not being afraid to ask

My first job was with Manfield Shoes in Oxford. I worked there every Saturday for five years.

I lived out in the sticks and the hourly bus to our village from Oxford left at twenty to the hour. I finished at 6:00 p.m.

Our manager set an incentive. The person who sold the most 'fancies' on a Saturday ('fancies' being shoe polish, laces, shoe trees and the like), got to go home half an hour early. If I achieved that, it meant that I was home a full hour early as a result of the bus times. This was a huge incentive to a teenager with money to spend.

I got that prize almost every Saturday for years. The reward, and the potential to get back to the village and impress girls, was highly motivating.

In later life, I ended up training shoe shop staff and talking about this very subject. Many clever techniques exist for introducing 'sundries' (as they're now called) to customers, but you know what works best?

Asking every person.

I believed, and could prove, that these products were beneficial to people's shoes. I believed that many of these products would enhance the look and extend the life of the shoe, ultimately saving the customer money. So I was really happy to sell them.

And you know what? If people say no to you, that's absolutely fine – and also helpful. It means that you know where you stand; you can stop following them up for now and take the relationship somewhere else.

One of the absolutely wonderful things about networking is that, generally, a 'no' today doesn't have to be a 'no' forever.

If you cold-call someone and they say 'no', you're never likely to get through again. This statement might be a generalisation but if someone has cold-called me and I've said 'no', I won't be available next time they call. I'm busy, as I'm sure you are, and if I've already decided about their product or service I don't need to spend time considering it again.

But if I'm at a networking meeting with them, seeing them for breakfast, lunch or dinner every couple of weeks, they might just be in the right place at the right time when my needs or my interest change.

Or I might spot that someone else in the room has bought from them, and that third-party endorsement might help me to rethink.

Following up might be as simple as carrying on going to the networking meeting where you originally met the prospect. It gives you the opportunity to continue to engage with them in a non-'salesy' way and it gives them the opportunity to see that you weren't just a flash in the pan and that you're there for the long term.

Asking for referrals

I talk here about asking for referrals from existing clients or prospects, rather than the wider subject of asking for referrals in the networking environment.

The first thing you need to do before asking for a referral is provide an awesome service.

This statement may seem obvious but many people miss it.

No matter what you're providing, over-deliver on service. Keep in touch with the client or customer; make sure that they love what you're doing. Doing so creates not just satisfied clients but also vocal advocates.

People love to tell their mates when they've experienced great value. If you're a graphic designer or copywriter or web designer, people want to show off what you've done for them. If you save people money or provide a better service on their insurance, people talk about you. If you provide any product or service and do it brilliantly, people talk about you.

This value has to come from you. You have to truly love and have passion for what you're doing.

Of course, the opposite is also true, which is why a networking event is a brilliant place to find suppliers as you can get honest feedback from other people in the room.

So, when you've over-delivered; when you've finished the design early and blown the client away with your ideas; when you've delivered the completed work to the client ahead of schedule, what then?

As ever, the simple answer is often the best. Something that works for many people goes along the lines of:

> 'Terry, I'm thrilled that you've been pleased with what we've done. It makes such a difference to us whenever clients tell us they appreciate us.
>
> I don't do any marketing except for networking or word of mouth. Do you know anyone else who I can talk to about what we do?'

Other people send a letter or postcard with the invoice, asking for referrals too.

Watch out for testimonials on social media. When someone takes the time to post a recommendation for you on LinkedIn or a testimonial on 4Networking or anywhere else, why not pick up the phone, thank them and ask them, right there and then, if they know anyone else who may need your service. Catch them right at the point at which they're having those favourable thoughts about you.

When he was developing 4Networking, Brad Burton would use what he called the 'Columbo Close'. He'd phone people up, invite them along to a networking event and, whether they wanted to come or not, at the end of the conversation, say 'just one more thing, do you know anyone else I should call?'

Every business is a business and every business person understands, or should understand, that stuff has to be sold.

4Networking chairman, Terry Cooper, sums it up for me: 'In over 40 years of selling, nobody has ever hit me when I asked for the order. Not once. Some people have said no, which is fine, and lots of people have said yes. But if all you're scared of is that someone might say yes or no, then you might as well get it out of the way now.'

Part III
Networking Online and Using Social Media

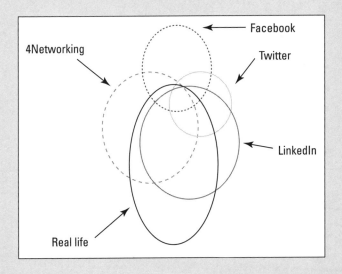

Go to www.dummies.com/extras/business networking for free online bonus content about making the most of business networking.

In this part . . .

✔ Discover the benefits of networking online and using forums.

✔ Find out why the personal touch is so important.

✔ Delve into the world of blogging.

✔ Choose the right social media platform for your business.

✔ Join up your online and offline networking.

Chapter 12

Networking Online

● ●

In This Chapter

▶ Networking online using business forums

▶ Choosing a forum (or forums) to suit you

▶ Realising why giving away your knowledge for free may be the best thing to do

● ●

*I*n the beginning of the Internet age, there were bulletin boards. Well, not quite the beginning, but the mid-1990s at least. Bulletin boards were an early form of community on the Internet where you could post stuff and people could respond. These boards were a really early form of social media, if you like. Bulletin boards existed when I first got a modem in around 1996.

Later came forums, and for every interest, however diverse, you can find a forum somewhere. You like *The Simpsons*? You can find forums where like-minded people discuss *The Simpsons*. You're into the world's finest and friendliest punk band, The Damned? Yep, you can find places on the Internet just for you. You want help mending your dishwasher? People are waiting on the Internet just to help you.

And if you're self-employed or run a business? You can find popular forums where you can get stuck in, virtually meet other business people, ask for help on business matters that may be new to you and generally chat and socialise too.

In this chapter we investigate why you may want to bother with business forums, where you can find them and what to do with them when you've found them.

Introducing Online Networking

I live in a small village in Oxfordshire. We have a population of about 1,200 people, two churches, a primary school, a shop, a post office, a pub and a garage.

Various people in various trades, professions and businesses live in the village.

I fictionalise the various characters in this story but say that Steve fits windows for a living, Victoria runs a company that provides payroll services to other companies and Paul is a coder, writing programs for other businesses. (All names have been changed to protect the innocent, and not so innocent.)

We villagers hold various village social events throughout the year. We have a fete, a school barbecue, a couple of village quiz nights and numerous productions by the school and local thespian society. On top of that, we have plenty of opportunities to meet other local people at the pub, the post office and just out and about in the village.

If I do bump into Steve at the village quiz, he generally doesn't ask me if I need any new windows fitted. Victoria doesn't immediately interrogate me on who I know who may need payroll services. Paul doesn't bombard me with suggestions as to how he can write software for my business.

Instead, we talk about stuff. We enquire about each other's lives and families. We discuss the planning application for a small development of houses on the outskirts of the village. We talk about the new people who've taken over the shop.

But if I ever wanted windows fitted, it would be Steve who I called on. If I come across one of my contacts who needs a payroll provider, I'd give them Victoria's contact details. That's what happens in a community, whether that community is a village, a society, a family or anywhere else where people interact.

 Online communities are often like villages. The people in the communities get to know each other, and build relationships and alliances. Sometimes, you become aware of in-jokes and unwritten rules as well as the published rules. They thrive on debate and occasional conflict. But they're also welcoming to newcomers too and in the lifetime of any forum, just like a village, a turnover of members occurs as people come and go.

Finding Business Networking Forums

Numerous business forums have sprung up around the UK. Each has its own character and style. Each has a different way of doing things and each has its own devotees. If you Google 'business networking forums', you can find a fair number.

Two of the more popular are:

- ✔ **4Networking** (of which I'm a director) www.4networking. biz/forum As well as being accessible to all the members of 4Networking's breakfast, lunch and evening groups across the country, 4Networking operates a forum that's free for any UK business owner to join and participate in. The 4Networking forum insists that every member publishes their real identity and contact details and the forum itself is lightly 'policed' with minimal rules and a chatty, light-hearted atmosphere.

- ✔ **UK Business Forums (UKBF)** www.ukbusinessforums. co.uk Claiming to be the 'UK's most active help and advice forum', UKBF certainly attracts a lot of copy-cat forums – none of which are as busy or have as many members. UKBF has both a free and paid-for membership, with members using nicknames on the forum and with a rigid and policed set of rules. Certainly a culture exists of members' questions being answered quickly by other members with a lot of great advice, and opinion, being given every day.

Aside from the two main players, loads more exist out there. It would be impossible, and wrong, to try to judge which is the 'best' – as with most things, you need to try a few for yourself and see which community you prefer.

 Incidentally, a lot of the groups on LinkedIn behave like online forums, so you can apply pretty much the same advice to these groups also.

Joining an Online Community

Joining the community is, in a lot of ways, the easy part. Most forums have a simple sign-up process, where you need to supply some information and receive your username (often your email address) and password. You can then start posting and joining in the discussions.

If you have an opportunity to complete an online profile, make sure that you do. You can supply information about your business, along with links and other information.

Also worthwhile, if the opportunity is there, is to provide a profile photo. People buy people and a photo appearing next to your posts helps others relate to you as a real person and not just a page on the Internet.

It may also be possible to add a 'forum' signature, which appears underneath every post you make, rather like an email signature. On some forums, this signature is only available to paid members, which gives you an idea of how valuable it is. Every time you post, details appear about your business, plus links back to your website.

Don't underestimate the value of any of these options.

Figure 12-1 shows some sample posts including photos and signatures.

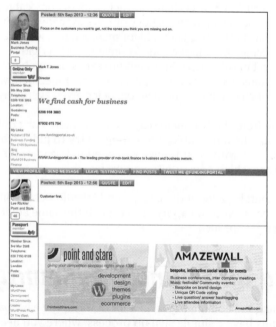

Figure 12-1: Typical posts from an online business forum.

Figure 12-2 is my forum profile from the 4Networking forum.

Figure 12-2: A profile page from the 4Networking forum.

If you're going to get stuck into online forums, make sure that you get your signature and profile set up first. Your signature and profile don't have to be immediately as professional as the ones shown, and your photo can be taken with your phone at first – although I'd strongly recommend getting a professional photo taken as soon as possible (it should cost you less than £50 and you can use your photo everywhere you promote yourself – a photo really is a worthwhile investment).

Think about what you want to write in your profile. In most industries and professions, you can use your profile to promote yourself and your business; in some professions, particularly financial services and the legal profession, you need to appreciate that this profile forms part of your advertising and is subject to the same regulation and compliance as anything else you do.

Becoming Part of Any Community

When you've completed your details, your time has come to become part of the community, meeting (virtually) the other members, introducing yourself and starting to participate in the community, as you would in real life. This point is where you need to remember my earlier 'village' analogy.

Many forums have a specific section where you can introduce yourself – on UKBF, this section is called 'Introductions' and on 4Networking we call it 'Say Hello'.

This place should be your first introduction; by all means say who you are and what you do, but resist the temptation to immediately start selling – you wouldn't do it the first night you walked into a new pub or the first time you met other parents at the school gates, so don't do it here. Most forums are extremely welcoming of new members, particularly those who take the trouble to introduce themselves.

When you've taken that first step, get stuck into the rest of the forum. Look at what discussions are taking place. Look at where you may be able to join in and add value. Often you can find general business discussions taking place, as well as subjects that may be specific to your sector – and of course you can also just chat.

Learn the mechanics of whichever forum or forums you choose, particularly how to make posts and how to know whether someone has replied.

If you do start posting, make sure that you check for replies and reply to them. It appears rude if someone starts a conversation and then doesn't take any part in it after that.

Don't feel that you have to immediately start posting. You can get at least as much value in replying to other members' posts; in effect joining in conversations rather than starting them.

One of the biggest truisms I've heard about online business forums is that to sell more, try selling less.

What does that mean in practice? Get to know people and allow them to get to know you. Demonstrate your expertise by joining in with the discussions and help other members out. Demonstrate your personality by getting involved with the chat and the community.

Advertising is Okay (Sometimes)

Every forum has a specific place for advertising your services or goods. Many people make the mistake of going in there first, going from zero to sell in their first post.

If you do that, nobody knows you. You've walked into the community and just left your leaflets there, hoping that people will buy from you. The people you want to buy from you, though, haven't had the chance to know you and, guess what, other people are around who provide the same service or product as you do. You won't find it uncommon for someone to post an ad as their first post and for nobody to even read it.

But you've read this book; you know that it's all about building the relationships first, getting to know the people and selling less to sell more.

You're in business to sell though and, judged correctly, the occasional advert can work exceptionally well.

If you spend time building the relationships and getting to know people, those same people will want to support you. If you spend time making interesting posts and comments, then other people in the community will look at your ad. They may be interested themselves, they may know somebody who is interested or they may help you by sharing your ad on other social media channels.

Getting to know people first, allowing them to get to know you, always provides better results than just posting from a cold start.

Most forums are attractive to Google and other search engines. The most attractive part of any post is the heading – a bit like the subject line in an email. While many books and publications exist that go into a great deal more detail on search engine optimisation – including the excellent *Search Engine Optimization For Dummies*, 5th Edition, by Peter Kent (Wiley) – if you want to draw attention to a page on your website, or a new offer you're promoting, then posting an advert with a carefully worded subject line and links within the text certainly helps Google find your original page.

Calling First Means That You Often Get the Job

Many forums have a section for people actively looking to buy other people's services. This section is usually called 'Can You Help?' or similar. In here, people often post looking for print services, or HR services, or for some banners ready for a show, or a courier to pick something up and move it around for them, or for a new website, or even search engine optimisation work on their existing website.

If you spot something of this kind and you think it relevant to you and your business, please resist the temptation to post 'We do that; call us for details' or similar.

No other sales environment exists that I know of where it would seem sensible to have a prospect approach you, give off loads of buying signals and then get the response, 'You do all the work and contact me so I can sell to you.'

Pick up the phone, chat to them about what they're looking for, build the relationship there and then and see what you can do to help, if you can fulfil what they're looking for. If you can, great; ask them whether you can go ahead.

If you don't offer what they're looking for, why not see whether you can refer them to someone who can? You won't have won the business this time, but you have done them a favour and saved them the trouble of looking.

Pick up the phone.

It may be that some of your contacts don't use Internet forums and you may sometimes spot something that could be a business opportunity for them. You can do yourself a lot of favours within your network by passing on potential leads that you spot. If I ever spot anything online, I paste the link into an email, Tweet or LinkedIn or Facebook message with a quick 'Saw this and thought of you' message. Genuinely caring about your friends' and contacts' businesses can be a brilliant way to build your reputation and profile as a networker and, as they say, what goes around comes around.

Establishing Yourself as the 'Go-To Guy' in the Community

Forums offer an exceptional opportunity to prove and demonstrate your expertise.

Although counter-intuitive, giving away your expertise freely on forums will get you more business. Telling people exactly how to do what you do, giving away most of your trade secrets, may seem like commercial suicide but is how some clever people market themselves online.

Even if you tell people how to do what you do, many people still want someone to do it for them. Even if you give people all the tricks and information to do their own search engine optimisation, or to take care of their own email marketing, or to design a world-leading brand identity, or to write excellent sales copy – many people want to pay for the service as they realise that, even with the knowledge, they don't have the expertise. And who are they likely to turn to? They may well turn to the person who has demonstrated that expertise and knowledge.

Look out for opportunities to show off just how much you know online. The more you demonstrate how much you know, the more the other people in the community come to know that and respect it – and this respect leads to one of the best things that can ever happen to your business. When someone posts in the Can You Help?, or similar, section of that forum, those same other people go in and recommend you first. Before you ever get to talk to the prospect, other people, independently, have recommended you.

You can even collect these recommendations, as many forums allow people to leave testimonials or endorsements for other members. So as well as your profile explaining how brilliant you are in your own words, you have third-party endorsements too – adding weight and credibility before a prospect for your services even talks to you.

Business forums are a microcosm, just like my small village in Oxfordshire. Some people you'll like and get on with; others you won't be sure about. Something that I've long since learned to do is to make the people real by picking up the phone and talking to anyone who I've engaged with online. Try it. You're there to network. You're there to build connections. In the village, you'd get to know the 'real' person over time. Internet communities need be no different.

Actually talking to people is often forgotten but is still the quickest way to build relationships. Written conversation, such as on online forums, is easy to misinterpret but speaking to someone helps to strengthen the relationship and gives you a much better insight into who the other person is.

In other words, a bit like real life.

Chapter 13

Using Social Media to Keep Relationships Alive

I truly wish that more businesses would see that the biggest opportunity in social media is in relationship building and not just prospect hunting. Too many businesses and business people still spend too much of their social media effort trying to sell to people, before finding out what they want to buy.

In this chapter I want to change your understanding of social media and give you some important and immediately useable hints and tips that help you to change the results you get from it.

Venturing into Social Media

I remember when an estate agency I was working for first had a website. This was in 1997 and the Internet was terribly exciting to us. We commissioned a company to design a site for us that we could upload our properties to and we spent hours working out what text to put on there. The copy on our home page told any visitor all about our firm, there was an About Us page telling people even more about how brilliant we were, and a page with photos of each member of staff with a little write-up about their experience and specialities.

It was a great website for 1997 and served the firm really well. We put the address on all of our stationery and proudly told potential clients that we were now on the Internet.

Being on the Internet was enough for 1997. The website itself was a broadcast of what was great about us and what was great about each property we were selling. That was what everyone was doing at the time. You got yourself a website saying how great you were, then you told people where to find it, so they could read how great you were too.

The world had speeded up a little. People no longer needed to wait until we advertised our properties every Friday afternoon – they could see them on the website as soon as we registered them. They didn't have to wait for us to post a set of details to them – they could read these on their screen and even print them out at home.

Realising that the times, they are a-changing

In the late 2000s, the Internet changed. As well as broadcasting at your visitors, it became possible for them to talk back to you. Clever people invented what became known as 'Web 2.0' and the world speeded up a little more.

Now not only could our potential clients and customers read our stuff on the Internet, but, as more and more people adopted social media, they could actually talk to us about it, engage with us and use social media as yet another communication channel.

The opportunity that far too many businesses still miss, is that the opposite also became true. It was now possible for us to engage with our prospective clients and customers; for us to find and talk to them without waiting for them to find out about us; for us to build relationships with people who may become client themselves or may know people who could become clients.

There was nothing new about this process. It was just networking as usual but using the various social media platforms as the medium of communication. Somehow the message that social media is just people talking to people is lost along the way, though, with too many social media accounts still stuck in 1997 'broadcast mode'.

Entering social media

I've had an account on Twitter since July 2008 and Facebook since August 2007. Some of my friends and followers have remained in place since I joined while others have come and gone, a little like in real life.

Social media makes it possible for you to build new relationships, continue existing ones, keep in touch with clients and contacts and, when you need to, draw attention to what you're selling.

Modern business networking combined with social media allows any business and any business person to assemble a crowd of people around them who, in time, may become clients, advocates, suppliers, referral partners, advisors or simply social contacts.

Winning Friends and Influencing People

It's often said that people like people who think like them. Everyone finds it easier to relate to someone who has something in common with them and, for anyone in sales or marketing (which is you by the way, because everyone is in sales and marketing), finding something in common is vital to building a relationship.

You can win friends by finding people with something in common with you. One of the absolute gifts presented by social media is that people talk about their interests out loud. You can actually see what people are interested in on their Twitter, Facebook, LinkedIn and Google+ timeline. They may even take photos of their interest on Instagram or Pinterest or even post their favourite videos on YouTube.

Finding common ground

Some people say that Twitter is a waste of time because all people do is talk about what they're having for breakfast or that they're 'walking the dog LOL'.

But what if they're having kippers and I like kippers too. I've got something in common with them! If I hate kippers with a passion, I have something to talk to them about as well.

What if I also have a dog? If someone tweets that they're walking the dog I can dismiss it as a waste of time, or I can ask them what type of dog they have, or, if they live locally to me, where they prefer to walk.

I have some old training books at home. They recommend that you really get to know your prospects and clients. They recommend that, if you keep your clients' details on index cards or in a Rolodex (I never did have a Rolodex and always felt left out when I read the books), you jot personal information on the back, such as their kids' names, what football team they support, what car they drive. That way you always have something to talk to them about, an excuse to call if their team wins a particular tournament or a point of commonality if your kids are similar ages, that sort of thing.

Social media has turbo charged this process. What would these old sales trainers have done with all the information we have to hand these days? Facebook tells me when my contacts' birthdays are. People tweet about which football team they're supporting, or how they feel about Vettel winning his fourth Formula 1 World Championship. People tell me what they're listening to or watching on the telly, and what they're doing for their kids' birthdays.

Forming meaningful relationships

With a plethora of information about our contacts and our crowd, you can easily find something in common with people and start to build relationships and friendships.

Think on the following. Robin Dunbar was a British anthropologist who observed a link between the size of each primate's brain and the size of their social groups. He applied that link, known as *Dunbar's Number*, to human brain size. Dunbar's

Number theory suggests that each human being can form meaningful relationships with 150 people at a time. But Dunbar came up with that theory in 1992, before social media had become mainstream. Dunbar's theory is based on maintaining relationships without the benefit of almost constant contact with the people in your circles. The potential for everyone to maintain multiple relationships is beyond the comprehension of previous generations but enables us to build the relationships that we've always known to be important, particularly in business.

With all of the potential contacts you can win and maintain by joining up social media with modern business networking, you can build yourself a huge sphere of influence; people who know you and trust you; people who look to you as a supplier because they already know you.

Going local, regional, national or international

People often evangelise the Internet and social media because it can get you a national or international reach and makes people all over the world potential connections and contacts. One of the benefits, we were told, of having a website in 1997 was that people all over the world would be able to look at it.

Many of the early videos and infographics about social media told us all about the scale. How many people per day were signing up to Twitter. How Facebook was now bigger than most countries when expressed in terms of the number of people on there.

But what if your business really does only serve people in your town, your county or the South of England? What if your business really can only cope with a few clients per week or per month. One of the dangers with how the Internet and social media is often 'sold' to people is that its very scale can be off-putting when you think it through. To put many people's thoughts into words, what's the point of me spending time building relationships with people all over the place when I only offer local delivery? What's the point of having all these contacts when actually I'm run off my feet right now, what with all the networking Stefan is telling me to do?

Social media enables you to keep in touch with people who are local to you, as well as changing what local means forever. Local to me is now more likely to mean those who I'm in daily contact with, instead of a geographical location. But if local to you means those people within 15 miles, or 75 miles, or 2 miles, then you must use social media to keep in touch with them too.

Social media even gives you the tools to find people who are local to you and engage with them too. Instead of advertising in your local newspaper and aggressively waiting for the phone to ring, you can now, if you want to, go straight to some local people and start engaging with them. You can even get notified when someone from out of town is visiting somewhere nearby!

Something else that was originally highly touted as a benefit of social media is that you can connect with 'celebs' like Richard Branson and Justin Bieber. But connecting with famous people usually serves nothing. Unless you really enjoy reading their tweets or posts, then concentrate on connecting with people who can genuinely form part of your crowd.

In books about business networking from only a few years ago, social media may have been mentioned as an afterthought, but in my opinion social media is the biggest change in how we maintain real-life relationships ever. Used correctly, social media is the biggest opportunity in business networking ever.

Joining in other people's conversations

You know that guy in the pub? The one who loves the sound of his own voice? They guy who only ever talks about himself?

How about that friend of yours who always tries to bring the conversation round to her and her interests? No matter what your kids have done, the conversation quickly becomes about her kids.

Try not to be that person on social media. You don't always have to talk about yourself, and you certainly don't have to continually broadcast about yourself or your business.

Instead of thinking about what you should say on social media, why not read other people's tweets and posts and consider them as the start of a conversation? Instead of talking about what's important to you, why not look at what other people are talking about, which is likely to be important to them, and engaging in conversation from there?

Consider other people's tweets and posts as an invitation to engage with them.

Staying in Your Contacts' Field of Vision

In the olden days, people worried about how to stay at the front of their customers' and prospects' minds.

No level playing field existed if you were a small company because the bigger companies had the advertising and marketing budget that provided the bigger and better opportunities to broadcast. Some companies even managed to associate their brands with annual holidays – that's why it's an advertisement for a sugary caffeinated drink that heralds the UK's biggest religious festival (advertising didn't always work commercially, of course, remember the spectacular and star-studded Woolworth's Christmas ads?).

Business networking starts with you making that first contact, that first handshake, that first exchange over breakfast, that first exchange of tweets or that LinkedIn connection request.

That's where it starts and, for too many people, where it also ends.

You never know when someone's going to need your services, or when someone's going to have a school gate or pub conversation with the person who'll become your next big client.

The trick, the biggest challenge for small businesses, the massive opportunity for clever networkers, is being there right at the moment when that thought is in someone's head – that they need someone who can supply your services.

Buy furniture!

Many people won't need your services when you first meet them. They may not know anyone who needs your services even after you've followed up.

Think about the 'End of Season Furniture Sale' adverts that you see on television. These companies don't just run the campaign once and hope that people remember the locations of their stores when they're ready to buy. They run the adverts constantly, in the knowledge that they'll be advertising in the middle of the programme you're watching, on the very weekend when you finally decide that your lumpy old sofa needs replacing.

Small businesses actually have an even bigger opportunity than the big companies now because, while the furniture companies are able to broadcast to us constantly, we're able to actually engage with our audience constantly. Not just telling them what we've got to sell at the moment but talking about the stuff that's important to them, while making sure that we constantly stay right at the front of their minds.

Lots of people say that they hate the furniture adverts, and that these days they just skip them using Sky+. But I bet that most of you reading this chapter have been to one of the stores that make the adverts. Those constant adverts work.

Building a proper and active social media following takes almost no money at all and actually can be done completely free. Compare that to what the furniture companies must have to spend on that constant TV coverage.

But why most small businesses give up is that building a following without a huge advertising budget takes time and effort – constant time and effort.

And just like that constant television spend by the furniture companies, and Coca-Cola, and many other companies, the return on investment from using social media is difficult or even close to impossible to immediately measure.

Going beyond: Following up with social media

After you've sent that LinkedIn connection request or followed someone on Twitter – what next?

Well, now, of course, you send them daily if not hourly links to what you do, your blogs, your stuff, invitations to buy, special offers and links to pages with your events on.

Right?

Wrong. Very, very wrong.

Now you talk to them. Show interest in their stuff. In fact, don't *show* interest in their stuff. *Be* genuinely interested in their stuff and what they're doing.

Be the nosy shopkeeper

In the olden days, if you owned a shop in a small town, it would be your business to know everyone else's business.

People may have thought that the old-fashioned shopkeeper was nosy, that he was a busybody, but he wasn't. It just made good business sense to know what was going on in the town.

If Mrs Smith came in the shop and you knew it was her birthday that week, you could congratulate her. If you knew that her son had just graduated, she'd be delighted that you mentioned it to her.

These conversations weren't about you being nosy; they were about building relationships with customers on their terms. Rather than just broadcasting what you were selling all the time, you had conversations about the things that were interesting to your shoppers.

If you've ever watched *Open All Hours*, you'll have spotted that Arkwright, the penny-pinching shopkeeper, was an absolute master of this kind of networking. Although the programme is a parody of the English 'corner shop', you'll see Arkwright asking about his customers' illnesses, along with knowing exactly what their shopping habits are. Arkwright made it his business to know about everyone else's business.

More recently, initiatives such as the Nectar card were introduced, supposedly to offer us discounts and money-off vouchers. But what the Nectar card and other similar initiatives really exist for is to build up a comprehensive record of who we are. The companies that offer these loyalty cards know what we buy every week and every Christmas, and whether we favour lager or white wine during the summer months. They know our birthdays and often our kids' birthdays too. They offer us extra points for filling in surveys that tell them when we're due to renew our home insurance.

Nectar uses the methods available to it to build a picture of our shopping patterns, just like Arkwright did by being nosy. Would Arkwright have loved the Nectar card? Hell, yeah. He just wouldn't have offered the money-off vouchers!

Keeping information at your fingertips

What if you had the opportunity to know pretty much everything about all of your contacts and how their lives and their businesses were developing and changing?

What if you knew whenever your contacts had a little business success – useful information if you're a business coach or sell congratulations cards? What if you knew when they took on new staff – useful if you offer human resources consultancy or insurance services? What if you knew they were moving into a new office – again, brilliant if you sell insurance, utilities or computer networking?

You see, all of this information about most of your contacts exists today, right now. And yet most people still use Twitter, LinkedIn and Facebook as a means to tell people what *they* are doing rather than to listen to what *other people* are doing, which is much more interesting to them.

Sensible networkers have to always be interested in the other guy, while at the same time presuming that everyone else is only interested in themselves.

Now, all of this taking an interest in people takes time and effort. But in the next sections I share some easy ways to keep on top of what your contacts are doing.

Thinking business? Think personal as well

Many people say that they like to keep their professional 'stuff' separate from their personal life and, for that reason, prefer to offer their LinkedIn connection to business contacts rather than their Facebook profile; people tend to see Facebook as more personal and LinkedIn as more about business.

However, that's thinking about it from your point of view, only considering what you're posting and talking about.

Consider connecting with your business contacts on Facebook and Twitter too. These sites are where they talk about their personal successes as well as their business updates, and are also where they tell you what their kids are up to and what they're doing for their birthday.

Regularly check the profiles of your LinkedIn contacts and see what's changed or what updates they've posted recently. If someone has a new position, why not 'Like' the post or, even better, write a quick comment congratulating her.

Do things differently

Do you want to really stand out? Why not do things differently, something your contacts really aren't expecting.

After breaking my ankle, I spent most of the summer of 2013 lying on a sofa at home unable to walk or drive. Feeling sorry for myself, I posted liberally about my woes on Facebook and Twitter, mainly hoping for sympathy – which I got.

But one person went the extra mile and is, as a result, forever fixed in my list of trusted contacts. A homeopath who I'd met at networking events in the East Midlands sent me some pills together with a personal letter and a leaflet with instructions on what to eat and what to do to help mend a broken bone. She sent this package without being asked to do so and without expectation of any sort of reward – although you can see a heartfelt recommendation for her from me on LinkedIn.

What was the cost? Maybe it was a few quid plus her time writing and posting the letter.

What was the reward? I'd never recommend another homeopath now. When someone shows that they're that caring, living their business that much, how can I possibly ignore them in future?

She acted on business information. And I've told the world about how brilliant she is.

A friend of mine was excited to be going on a skiing trip for the first time in years. A personalised gifts company simply posted her a tube of lip salve, with their branding on it. What was the cost? It was pretty much zero apart from a few minutes of someone's time. What was the reward? My friend talked about it all over Twitter and Facebook, thanking the person for being so kind.

The homeopath was already a contact of mine. The person-alised gifts person was already a contact of the friend who went skiing – but look at what they did to the relationship just by listening and then acting, in a really imaginative way, on what they'd heard.

Do you send Christmas cards to your customers, clients, prospects and suppliers? Why not do something a little bit different?

 Try sending them a birthday card when Facebook tells you it's their birthday. Not a free e-card with a jingle, but a real card; write it by hand and post it a few days in advance.

What about if one of your clients is sick? Send them a get well soon card, or fruit, or flowers.

Instead of your card getting lost in the plethora of Christmas cards they receive, by doing something on another occasion you can really stand out.

And guess what, people tell you when their birthday is, when they're ill, when their wedding anniversary is, and lots of other invitations for you to congratulate them on, on Twitter and Facebook. You only have to listen.

What if your best client (or prospect or supplier) posts on Facebook that their wedding anniversary is coming up and they're going to a particular restaurant that night to cele-brate? What would your relationship be like the following day if they arrived to find a bottle of champagne on ice from you?

I've yet to think through what happens if everyone follows this advice. I am, of course, looking forward to posting which restaurants I'm going to after writing this book and then find-ing the place full of champagne from grateful readers!

One of my staff at 4Networking posted on Twitter recently that she really wanted a particular chocolate bar but hadn't been able to get to the shops to buy one. The next day a box full of assorted chocolates, including her favourite, was delivered to her office.

It cost me about £20.

What was the reward? She posted lots on Facebook and Twitter about how she has the 'best boss ever'.

Discarding your doubts

Does this advice all sound a bit wacky and out there to you? Are you reading this thinking, 'That'll never work'? Go on, admit it.

However, you're thinking about this matter from your point of view, the sender. Think about it from the other side of the fence. Think about getting to that restaurant and finding a bottle of champagne and a little card saying 'Hi Charlie, spotted on Facebook you were celebrating tonight and hope you don't mind me adding to your celebration. Have a great night.'

How would you feel? I bet you'd be straight on the phone to that contact the next day to thank them. I bet you'd tell everyone about it as well.

My 'thing' is punk and rock gigs and, as I write, I'm about to go out tonight to an Adam and the Ants reunion gig in London. I have free tickets as some mates of mine are the support act.

Lee, who handles my online presence, is also an old punk and lives in North London. I could have just got enough tickets for me and my friends but how pleased do you think he is that I'm giving him a night out on me?

I know that Lee @PointAndStare is a punk because he's taken the time to engage with me on Twitter and talk about the gigs that I go to. He's shared some of the music that he's into and given me advice and websites to look at for my son's embryonic career as a musician.

Any business benefit here? Well, I didn't start by thinking about that. I just knew he'd like a ticket. But Lee is a massive advocate of my stuff, always comes to my speaking gigs when I'm in London *and* was the first person to pre-order this book. He got in before my mum, my grandmother, my grandmother's parish priest and my grandmother's friends in Dublin – pretty good going as they were on it as soon as it became available for pre-order on Amazon.

When you show genuine interest in the other person, really listen to what's important to them and react to that, they can become advocates for life.

Spotting easy referral opportunities

So, you follow two people on Twitter or Facebook.

One is a supplier of remote IT services, helping and supporting people with their IT, networking and computer needs. The other is a graphic designer whose business is currently growing.

One day the graphic designer moves to a bigger office so as to be able to provide space for the two extra staff he's employed. You're following his move on Twitter, and have already sent him a 'new home' card because you read the previous pages in this book and took my advice.

At about 2:00 p.m. on the day of the move, his tweets become increasingly littered with expletives. At 2:20 p.m. you catch a tweet that reads along the lines of 'I'm going to throw this *** laptop out of the *** window if it doesn't talk to the network in the next five *** minutes.'

Pick up the phone. Right now. Do it. Introduce him to your IT support mate and see if the two can be put in touch and one help the other out in their hour of need.

Then tweet them and say words to the effect of '@ITGUYMARK meet @OpusCreativeDB – hope you two have got it sorted!'

From listening to what's going on on social media and reacting to it, you've made two people's days, and all for a few minutes' work and a couple of phone calls.

Getting Maximum Value from Blogging by Hardly Writing a Word

Everyone in business should blog. Whether they write down words or use YouTube, SoundCloud or similar to record their thoughts is irrelevant, but if you're passionate about what you do, then talk about it and tell people how passionate you are.

But writing blogs is only one half of the story. Someone has to read blogs and, if you want your stock value with your contacts to rise, you need to read, share and comment on others' blogs too.

Have you ever written a blog and then sat there and wondered if anyone read it or liked it? Oscar Wilde got it right, in the days before blogs, when he wrote: 'There is only one thing in the world worse than being talked about, and that is *not* being talked about.'

When you've crafted your blog and nobody comments, when virtual tumbleweed blows through your WordPress village, you feel lonely and think that nobody cares.

You have the opportunity to save your contacts from feeling this woeful *and* you might learn something from their blog too.

So, when you next see a tweet or a LinkedIn update from a contact, prospect, supplier or client, with a link to their blog, do the following:

- ✔ Take two minutes to read it. Most blogs aren't more than a few hundred words so won't take that long to read.

- ✔ If you like it, comment and say so, then retweet or share it.

- ✔ Don't just do that once, or just a few times and decide I'm stupid for suggesting it and don't know what I'm talking about. Keep doing it, as a matter of course.

When you tweet things, you put your thoughts out there, and you want other people to read and like what you've done.

Keep reading people's blogs. By showing that you're truly interested in what your contacts have to say, you:

- ✔ Reinforce your relationship with them

- ✔ Learn from their blogs

- ✔ Give yourself something else to tweet about or share on LinkedIn without having to write content yourself

- ✔ May even get retweeted or shared yourself if other people like your contact's blog

- ✔ Give yourself nuggets of inspiration for your own blogs and posts

I share lots of other people's blogs and comments, particularly on LinkedIn and Tumblr. As well as helping whichever contact wrote the blog, doing so brings more value to the rest of my crowd, and followers too, and I'd be delighted if one of my contacts got business as a result of me sharing their stuff.

Whatever your own business is, you can derive huge benefits from sharing content from other people in the same industry. Becoming a 'curator' of useful (and even useless) information about your industry and talking about it makes you a useful commentator and builds your reputation as an expert in your field. I know people who, as a result of always commenting on other people's content, are now asked to comment on their subject on local and national radio.

Bear in mind the old adage, 'If you don't have anything nice to say, don't say anything at all.' If you're happy to be controversial online and prepared for the kickback, fine, but if not, think hard before posting negative comments on people's blog posts or other content.

Curating information about your industry or profession

If you read widely about developments in your profession or industry, try starting conversations based on articles you've read in newspapers or on LinkedIn or anywhere else you spot something that interests you. For example:

✔ If you're an estate agent, myriad articles and discussions about house prices and the Help to Buy Scheme are doing the rounds.

✔ If you're an interior designer, every week you can find related articles in the weekend supplements, giving you the opportunity to comment on the merits of each project.

✔ If you're a writer, books and articles are published in their thousands every week, giving you the opportunity to comment on and share what you like with your tribe.

You can stay in touch with your contacts, and be seen as an authoritative voice on any subject you choose to by reading, commenting and sharing.

This morning I read an article about public speaking in *The Observer*, liked it and quickly shared the link on Twitter, Facebook, LinkedIn, Tumblr and Google+. Within half an hour, I was engaged in conversation with other people about it. The thing is, they're relating that article and that information to me now.

Get Evernote, or Google Keep, or a way of saving stuff and notes which works for you. I use Evernote and, when I spot something I like, I use one of the apps to save the article there and then. I now have an ever-growing encyclopaedia of information and resources on business, public speaking and the like, always ready to share if people ask me. All of this information is searchable and stored forever, along with the link back to the original article.

If you're going to share other people's stuff, as I do, make it clear that it's someone else's, as I do. Sharing a link to the original article is good. Copying, pasting and passing it off as your own is bad.

Whenever you need personal inspiration for a blog, have a look through the stuff you've saved, see what you like, can use for inspiration or can comment on.

If you share someone else's stuff on social media, see whether you can tag them on Facebook or LinkedIn or @ them on Twitter. They're likely to share your share of their stuff (still with me?) plus they very often thank you and connect with you too, bringing someone else into your circle of contacts.

If you like someone's stuff that much, send them a Tweet or LinkedIn message and tell them so, making sure that you tell them specifically what you liked. They'll love the positive feedback!

Remembering it's about conversation not content

A good piece of advice, no matter which social media platform you're using to keep in touch with your contacts, is to forget about broadcasting and start engaging.

Instead of deciding you only want to stick with Twitter and LinkedIn, think about where your contacts are and go there. Yes, you need to make more effort than sticking with what you know, but if your best prospect really loves Pinterest or Tumblr, wouldn't it make sense to go onto their turf and engage with them where they're comfortable?

Broadcasting, in many ways, is yesterday's approach and an old-fashioned methodology. The ability to engage and actually talk to your constituency is an approach that takes more immediate effort than broadcasting but ultimately leads to much larger rewards.

I think that people often broadcast on social media because it ticks a box. When they've tweeted or posted something, they think that's the job done (in some cases, people have employed someone else to handle their social media and tweeting for them is what they're paying for). This exercise isn't about box-ticking, though, and if you treat it as such, you're going to lose out.

I use the word 'constituency' quite a lot when I'm talking about networking and social media and I see lots of parallels here with how politicians gain ground over each other.

Think about the similarities.

When an election is coming up, the profile of your local politician and his competitors rises exponentially. They may have been a bit quiet for the last four years but now they have something to sell to you and they want to get your attention:

- ✔ So you start getting leaflets through the door – that's the marketing box ticked.

- ✔ They find people who are willing to stick a poster in their window or, even better, on a tall stake in the garden. Excellent, that's the third-party endorsement box ticked.

- ✔ They may even phone you, or come and knock on your door and talk to you for a bit, finishing with the world's worst closing comment, 'Can we count on your support?' That's the 'engagement' box ticked.

However, what if they really engaged with their constituents for the whole four years between elections? What if they really talked to people constantly and noticed what their constituents were doing rather than focusing just on what they themselves want – your tick against their name when you're alone in the polling booth?

If a politician, local or national, paid that sort of attention to their constituency, honestly and constantly, he'd probably win lots of votes, not least because people would feel like they knew the politician as a person. That sort of engagement is powerful and is exactly what I'm suggesting you employ as you grow your circles of networking contacts and keep those relationships alive using social media.

Don't be the person who's only there when you've got something to sell, or is there and selling all the time. Be the person who's always there listening, engaging and being genuinely interested in what the other person needs, over and above what you need.

Then, when you have something to sell, people want to help you, to support you, to buy your stuff or find other people who do. That sort of engagement is powerful beyond measure. Most people claim they don't have the time. Be the person who does. That way, you stand out.

Chapter 14

Networking Using Different Social Media Platforms

In This Chapter

▶ Choosing the right platform for your business

▶ Networking on Facebook, Twitter and other platforms

▶ Writing blogs and more

*T*he sheer volume of social media channels is so huge that some people simply choose not to bother networking using social media because they believe that they only have time to do one or two and that will be pointless.

The good news is that you can choose the channels that work for you and stick with them. In this chapter, you find out how to choose the right platform for your business, as well as the ins and outs of each one.

Choosing the Right Platform for Your Business

Choosing the right channel actually reflects some old-fashioned advice, but just applies this to the digital world.

In the olden days, if you wanted to network with accountants, you'd find out where lots of accountants were and go there.

The basic logic here remains the same. Who do you want to network with? Which social media channels are they using? Go there.

Being in the right place

When I started my career, a lot of people I wanted to network with played golf. In the old world, you were told that a lot of business was done on the 19th hole; that if you wanted to meet the right people, you needed to be on the golf course.

As estate agents in a small town in Oxfordshire, it was vital to us that we attended anywhere where lots of other local people hung out. The chamber of commerce breakfast meetings were essential for us, and me and my boss at the time were involved in various local social organisations. We wanted to meet and engage with people who owned houses locally, and might one day want to sell them, so we went to the places where they'd congregate.

Two golf lessons in the driving rain convinced me otherwise, frankly. I have huge respect for people who enjoy golf. I simply didn't. Plus the trousers never suited me.

Note, though, that you shouldn't just choose the channels that you're personally comfortable using. You need to find out where your prospects and contacts hang out and go to that place, in a digital sense.

When any new social media channel launches, I'd recommend you 'land grab' your brand on there, even if you aren't going to use it straight away. Most social media channels are free to join, so grab your company name before anyone else does, then seek advice on whether the channel is the right place for you.

In the following sections, I explore some of the more popular social media sites.

Twitter

Often when people talk about social media, what they actually mean is Twitter. Described as 'SMS for the Internet', Twitter is, these days, a constant stream of conversation between users, played out in 140-character tweets.

I love Twitter. I love the immediacy, the speed of conversation, the fleeting nature of most tweets, so that you can dip in and out – and the conversation, or millions of conversations, simply keep flowing.

At the time of writing, 218 million active Twitter accounts are reportedly in existence, and Twitter is definitely the *de facto* social media, where, I'd argue, any and every business now needs to have a presence.

Twitter, in my opinion, is the hub for most of your other social media activity too.

Keeping in touch with Twitter

Here are a few ways to use Twitter to keep in touch with your contacts:

✔ Make sure that your contacts know your Twitter handle/ name/alias. Mine is @NoRedBraces and is plastered all over everything I do, including my business cards and any signature or profile anywhere on the Internet. As soon as people follow you on Twitter, you can introduce them to your other social media profiles too.

✔ Ensure that your Twitter profile is complete, along with a link to your website or blog. Try to make your bio engaging, telling people enough that they want to find out more.

✔ Watch your timeline for people tweeting links to their blogs or other content. If you've got time, have a read, then retweet the links, along with a comment if you're able to using Hootsuite or one of the smart phone Twitter apps.

✔ Answer people when they tweet questions and particularly if they @ you (when someone replies to you or mentions you, as opposed to sending a direct message, you get an @ in front of your Twitter name). Get engaged in conversations.

✔ Set Twitter up to notify you by email when certain things happen, like someone follows you or retweets one of your tweets. The settings are in `https://twitter.com/ settings/notifications`. When someone takes the time to follow you or retweet you, send a quick tweet thanking them.

✔ Use Twitter's brilliant search facility at `search.twitter. com` to find people talking about stuff related to your profession or industry. Twitter even has an advanced search page where you can be incredibly specific and search on particular topics, tweets about a certain person, or even tweets originating from a particular place.

Tweeting secrets

Whenever I'm sat at my laptop, I have a search page open for the term 'business networking'. I often find new blogs being tweeted about that I can read and new people that I can engage with. When you spot something that you like, follow the person who tweeted and @ them, telling them what you liked about it.

If you've a referral for someone, tweet @ them with it. Even introduce the other person to them using their Twitter handle.

If you spot a link on a forum or elsewhere on the Internet that may be an opportunity for one of your contacts, tweet @ them with the link and say why you thought it may be of interest. It's immediate, simple and keeps you in contact; it helps out your contacts and builds your reputation as someone who looks for opportunities for others.

Every time you do this, people look at your profile. Every time you give people something of interest or value, the trail leads back to you. Every time you put something on Twitter, what you write can be read by the whole world.

If you want to @ someone on Twitter but want the tweet to be visible to everyone else, put a single character and a space in front of the @. If you @ someone, by default that tweet only appears on the timeline of people following both of you. If you put a single character in front, Twitter puts it on the public timeline.

Putting in the time and effort

Twitter takes time and effort, and the time and effort must come from you. In my opinion, Twitter isn't the place to employ someone to tweet on your behalf, or to set up software to tweet for you. Tweeting is a conversation, not a broadcast. The skill is much more in the listening than the talking. Someone clever once said, 'you have two eyes, two ears and one mouth; use each in the correct proportion'. Never is that truer than on Twitter.

You wouldn't send someone into a networking event on your behalf. You wouldn't simply post a load of leaflets to a networking event and expect people to take notice. The only difference with Twitter is the means by which you communicate, not the communication itself.

Facebook

You probably already have a personal Facebook account and a Facebook page for your business. Facebook users can like your business page, and you can post information, blogs, offers and the like.

The pace of Facebook, your personal profile or your business page, is a little more relaxed than Twitter, and with space to say more than the 140 characters that Twitter allows.

The best value from Facebook (ignoring Facebook ads for now) lies in reading what other people have posted, whether business or personal. Take the time to read, comment on and share the stuff you like on Facebook. If someone starts a conversation and you reckon you can add value, or just thank them for what they've said, then join in.

If you spot something that you know someone else will like, or you spot something about them or their business on the Internet, take the time to post it on their profile or wall, or use Facebook's tagging facility to tag them in any post.

When you post on Facebook, it allows you to tag other people or pages that you're connected to. As you start typing a name on Facebook, the program tries to fill in the rest of the name based on the people you're connected to. If you let it fill in the correct name, you see that name emboldened on your post, plus it notifies that person that you've mentioned them, further encouraging them to engage.

When Facebook has completed filling in the person's full name, you can delete the surname and leave the first name in place. Unless you typically refer to your friend as 'Jane Smith', using just the first name makes the post read much more naturally.

If you do have a distinction between your business page and personal profile, make sure that they don't share everything you post. If I like your page and am friends with you, I don't need to see the same thing on my timeline from both accounts. If you make a distinction, stick with the distinction, otherwise you're making it too easy for people to decide to only follow one.

LinkedIn

LinkedIn is the place to be if you're a professional anywhere in the world and want to connect and keep in touch with other professionals. I can't really say whether LinkedIn is the Facebook for business or whether Facebook is the LinkedIn for people, but the power of LinkedIn to keep your networking connections live must not be ignored.

LinkedIn also offers you a personal profile and business page option, but the focus even on the personal profile is on your business and career rather than your holiday photos and day-to-day musings.

To make it work for you, you need to encourage conversation on LinkedIn. Write regular updates and posts in such a way that you encourage other people to engage with them. Once people are engaged in the conversation they're much more likely to share your post with others, plus it gets you talking to them and you've chosen the agenda for them to talk about.

LinkedIn gives you a huge opportunity, used correctly, to identify yourself as an authority and as someone with a valid opinion about your subject.

Join groups where people are talking about the subjects you're interested in and engage with the conversations on there. You can find a ready supply of new contacts in these groups and you can start from a position of having something already in common – you presumably have both joined a group because you're interested in that subject.

If you spot something someone has posted in a group that you really like, as well as commenting publicly, send them a private message telling them why you liked it and, if you're not already connected, invite them to connect with a personal note.

LinkedIn Today (`www.linkedin.com/today/`) is a massive resource of interesting articles and blogs, shared from all over the Internet. If you're looking for interesting stuff to share and start conversations about, or join in conversations about, LinkedIn Today is a brilliant place to start.

LinkedIn search also enables you to search for people who work for certain companies, have particular keywords in their profiles, live in certain geographic locations and all sorts of other criteria. Some features of the search are only available to 'Premium' (that is, paid for) LinkedIn members, so you need to decide whether the extra functionality is worth it for you.

The pace and tone of LinkedIn is different to Twitter and Facebook. Set yourself a small amount of time every day to comment or post on LinkedIn, or add something to your professional profile or portfolio – what you post appears on your contacts' timelines. LinkedIn isn't a constant conversation like Twitter, but is a conversation nevertheless.

Google+

In many ways a new kid on the block, and with a different take on social media, Google+ further blurs the distinction between whether your social media presence is business or personal.

As the key difference with Google+ is the way it allows you to organise your contacts into circles, spend a little bit of time doing so. Any contact can be in as many circles as you like, but you may find sorting people according to the stuff that interests them worthwhile.

When you post on Google+, you're allowed to choose which of your circles the post is visible to. You can choose multiple circles, so you've a great deal of opportunity for overlap.

For example, if I find something about business networking, I may share it with my circle entitled 'Networking'. I share things on the basis that I hope that anyone involved in networking as part of their business will be interested in improving their networking skills. Of course, if everyone involved in networking purchased this book, that would be a start.

Just as with the other media, take the time to read other people's stuff. You can use the +1 button to show your appreciation of anything that grabs your attention.

At the time of writing, lots of people haven't yet got to grips with Google+. However, it's here to stay and some people are already huge advocates, so persevere with it.

One of the most overlooked and yet powerful tools in Google+ is Google Hangouts. You can set up a hangout with any other users who have a webcam and microphone. Google Hangouts is becoming popular as both an alternative to Skype and as a way of setting up an informal gathering of people in disparate locations.

Blogs

For many people, the blog is the heart of their social media activity. If you want to pass knowledge onto your followers, then your blog can sit in the middle of the operation, and you can ultimately share your blog content throughout your Twitter, Facebook, LinkedIn and Google+ timelines.

You can use various blogging platforms, such as WordPress, Tumblr, Blogger and Medium.

With any blogging, think first about why you're doing it. Are you imparting knowledge to others? Are you looking to build a crowd of followers who like your 'stuff'? Are you establishing yourself as an expert in your field?

Make sure that your writing inspires people to respond and to build up dialogue with you. If people are responding, you receive feedback, which may be valuable. And dialogue gives you an opportunity to express your opinion. Having an opinion on your subject, even if controversial, helps people understand what you stand for.

As soon as you blog, make sure that you share the content with other platforms to give your blog the widest possible readership.

Instagram

Instagram (owned by Facebook) is a bit like Twitter but for photos and videos. An incredibly useful way to let people into your life and your interests, Instagram has apps for iPhones,

Android phones and Windows phones that can help you quickly take and edit a photo or short 16-second video and share it with the world.

You can automatically share to your Twitter, Facebook, Tumblr and Foursquare account from within the app.

Vine

Vine concentrates on what it does best, which is tiny, seven-second video clips. Also, with apps for many smart phones, Vine forces you to think about how to get your message over in short bursts. Owned by Twitter, Vine has inspired a lot of incredibly creative seven-second clips.

If you're blogging, think about your headline or soundbite. Use Vine or Instagram to quickly record and get it out there on other social media. Add a comment with a link to the blog.

Foursquare

I like Foursquare. Getting used to the 'point' of it takes time but this platform is incredibly useful, particularly if you're a local business.

Foursquare allows you to share the locations you visit plus add photos. I use Foursquare to 'check in' to the locations of many networking meetings I'm attending and share that to Twitter and Facebook.

A huge benefit of Foursquare is that it allows you to see who's checking in close by to you. If I'm at a large-scale business show, I can see (and connect and engage with) the other people who are checked in there too.

If you're a business that only supplies locally, Foursquare can let you know of anybody who's close by. I was once in Gerrards Cross and checked into a networking meeting there. A local deli spotted me checking in, engaged with me on Twitter and suggested that I go in there to buy my lunch. I didn't have a better offer and I felt sort of obliged as they'd taken the trouble to engage with me. Bothering to check their timeline and reply to me took a couple of minutes of their time. I spent just under £10 on what I'm sure was a slow Tuesday for them.

Pinterest

Pinterest works on a graphically attractive platform, based loosely around the idea of 'pinning' your ideas to 'boards'. Think of a corkboard in your kitchen where you stick your best ideas, but in Pinterest's case, you've got a load of people in your kitchen looking at your board and you can see theirs too.

On top of this, you can set up several boards for different interests and you can follow a board, or all the boards, created by one person.

Hardly surprisingly, for a graphical interface, much of the activity on Pinterest is graphic, so using it, if your business interests aren't graphic, takes imagination.

You build community on Pinterest by following those people with similar interests to you, and repinning, sharing and liking other people's pins. You can also comment on and join in with other people's conversations. Think hard about Pinterest. Think about creating visual diaries of your work or pinning images with salient points if you write or present.

Taking the Next Steps in Social Media

I could easily write a whole book telling you which buttons to press on each social media platform, but for many people that really isn't the point. If you can see, from what I write about here, why you should use some of these platforms, the how becomes simpler, as you become motivated to do so.

Social media is an extension of your real-life networking. If you're inspired to want to look further into any of these platforms, start with the authoritative *Social Media Marketing For Dummies*, 2nd Edition, by Shiv Singh and Stephanie Diamond (Wiley), which goes into a lot more detail on each of the platforms.

Behind every keyboard is a real person. Every real connection has value to you and to them. Consider what value you can bring to them, just like in any other networking environment. Which platform you choose to do that through is irrelevant; just get busy building your crowd through engagement and demonstrating that you care.

Chapter 15

Joining Up Your Online and Offline Networking

*T*he opportunities for you to network have never been greater – both online and offline. In the olden days (about three years ago), you might network one morning a week. You might have the occasional social get-together as well but, broadly speaking, your networking was limited to when you were in the same room as a load of other people networking.

Now, however, networking is a constant activity. As well as face-to-face networking, your contacts, prospects, suppliers, referral partners, friends and *competitors* are networking online. Networking is now as much about an attitude as an activity. Networking involves you being there, among the crowd, creating your crowd, as much as you possibly can. These are really exciting times for businesses.

Acknowledging that People are People – However You Connect

I know that some of you don't 'do' Twitter, Facebook or LinkedIn. I also know that some of you who do 'do' these platforms think that getting someone else to send the odd tweet out for you or having a static profile on LinkedIn is enough. You've ticked a box. You're 'on' social media. So that's taken care of.

But it isn't. Just because you don't 'do' social media, doesn't stop your contacts doing it. This chapter is probably the most passionate in the whole book because so many people are ignoring what's really going on out there, and ignoring extended networking at their peril.

Just because you're not there doesn't mean that the conversation is going to stop and wait for you. Your contacts, clients, prospects and competitors are carrying on the conversation without you.

Businesses, and particularly small-business owners, must realise that the level playing field they've wanted for so long now exists. And the playing field is *level*. That means that everyone else is on there too.

People often tell me that they don't have time to be networking and on social media as much as I am. People tell me that they have 'real work' to do. And people also tell me that they don't know how I find the time to be out networking and on social media and ever do any real work!

The answer is that I find the time because networking on and off social media is *so* important. Never before have you had such an opportunity to connect with everyone you want to and be a part of the crowd, or, indeed, lead the crowd if you really put the effort in.

I often ask people who tell me they don't have the time, what's more important to be spending time on than talking to customers and contacts? What can be more important than extending your reach into more and more communities?

Going to networking events and continuing those relationships on social media is a part of modern business and even more so for the small-business owner.

Finding Your Strongest Connections

Who are the people who are most connected to you? Who are the people you're more than just a connection to on social media; people whose businesses you really understand and know exactly what sort of referral would be brilliant for them? Whose sense of humour do you 'get' and know exactly what light-hearted stuff to send to them? Who constantly retweets your stuff and seems to really buy into what you're doing?

If you don't know, find out!

Take a look through your Twitter timeline. Who are you actually interacting with? Who do you make a point of replying to? Think about LinkedIn and Google+. Whose posts do you actually enjoy reading and look forward to?

What about your contacts from your networking group? Who do you look forward to an informal drink with? Who do you pick up the phone to if you're having a rubbish day and just want to offload?

Think about the circles within circles too. Figure 15-1 illustrates what most of our lives look like (if you choose to express your life in a primary school-style Venn diagram!).

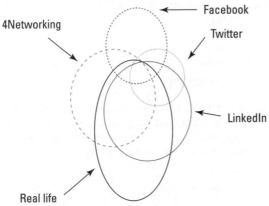

Figure 15-1: Circles within circles.

Taking advantage of tools to connect

You can even find tools to help you look at how connected you are with people online, for example:

- **Klout** (www.Klout.com). I like Klout. I completely get why people say that you can't measure your online presence in the way that Klout tries to with a simple score, but I also recognise that Klout has other tools that are useful. For example, if you sign up to Klout, on your profile page (http://klout.com/NoRedBraces), it shows you who's interacting with your tweets and updates as well as who appears to 'influence'

you; that is, who you choose to engage in dialogue with.

- **Vizify** (www.vizify.com). Vizify actually gives you a circles-within-circles-type diagram showing you who you most commonly interact with. It even animates the diagram to show you how people move closer to you and away from you over time.

- **Twitter.** Log into Twitter and go to https://twitter.com/i/connect and it shows you who's been retweeting you and interacting with you online.

Who are you connected with *everywhere*? Who are you in daily if not hourly contact with and know exactly what's going on in their life and business?

Who's right in the middle? Whose relationships with you join up in several places? These people may not even be doing business with you right now but I bet they know a lot about your business.

The point isn't just to know that these people exist, but to think about what you're doing, today, right now, to keep those connections alive.

Use this information to know where you're making a difference and who is currently part of your crowd. Then make sure that you join up your real life and online interactions to strengthen the relationship at every opportunity.

Meeting People Before You Meet Them

I've talked mainly about connecting in real life with your contacts *after* you've engaged with them in real life but the opposite is also possible and extremely worthwhile.

Used creatively, social media can make sure that you *never* walk into a room full of strangers again.

If you know that you're going to a networking meeting outside your normal area, then get on Twitter as far in advance as possible and start asking if anyone else is going. Also go onto the forum or website for that networking event and check out if the regular members talk about it online (in 4Networking, you can go directly to the Group/Events Happenings & News part of the forum).

If the event has a forum post or similar, get stuck in and tell people who you are and when you're attending. Every networking event everywhere loves to welcome new people, so take the opportunity here to build rapport with a few regulars. At the least, they then know to expect you and you will feel a connection with some of them immediately. This making contact also greatly shortens the process of people getting to know and trust you as much of the 'small talk' can take place before you actually meet and, if you've something in common, you may have found that out too.

I was to speak at the Business Growth Show in Manchester in 2010 and, at the time, knew hardly anyone up there. I spent time beforehand finding people who were talking about the event using `search.twitter.com` and, by the time I arrived at the venue, I'd found people who I felt a real connection with. Instead of speaking to an audience full of strangers, I already had several people in the room who had greeted me with a smile and told me they were looking forward to hearing me speak. Just imagine how much more pleasant that is than not having any friendly faces in the room at all.

Researching your prospects

People talk on social media. That's what it's for. People talk about what's going on in their life and their business like never before.

Have you ever been embarrassed to pitch to a prospect and find out that you've managed to completely misunderstand what they're trying to achieve? I have. It isn't fun when you're sat there.

Have you ever wished that you could have known more about a prospect before talking to them?

If a prospect contacts you and wants to talk about what you can offer, you have an opportunity to research them in advance and find out more about them and their company than you could ever have done before social media.

- ✔ Do the obvious and look at their website, read up about what they already offer and who some of their clients are.

- ✔ Search on social media for the person who contacted you and make sure that you connect on LinkedIn, Facebook, Twitter and Google+.

- ✔ If their website has a list of staff members, then search their names and connect with them too.

- ✔ Has the company got a page or group on LinkedIn or Facebook or a community on Google+? If so, like it or join it.

- ✔ Take time to note what people are talking about, what interests they have and anything they're moaning about that may be relevant to you.

- ✔ Listen before you speak. Understand as much as possible about what they need before you even meet them.

Is some of what you're reading in this chapter a bit 'out there' and you're not sure whether you can really do it in real life? Stop thinking from your side of the desk.

People regularly approach me with 'the next huge idea' for 4Networking. Often, all too often, this idea turns out to be something we're already doing. About once a month, an outside company approaches me saying, 'Wouldn't it be brilliant if you had a website where your members could network in-between meetings' – proving that they haven't even done the most basic research into how our network and business works.

How much more impressed would you be to get a call from someone who'd taken the time to really understand what you do in advance of contacting you?

How pleased would you be to hear from a LinkedIn contact in real life? How thrilled would you be if you were attending a networking meeting in a strange town for the first time and one of the local members called you a few days in advance to introduce themselves?

Go the extra mile. Be the person who does the things that nobody else bothers to do. Think carefully about how to join up your relationships and make you stand out.

Listening online, then speaking on the phone

Do people forget that they do still actually have the option of picking up the phone and talking these days?

Think about this option for a second and then do me a favour and make a commitment to doing it. Respond by phone every so often. That's right, spot something on social media and respond by picking up the phone and talking to that person:

- ✔ One of your contacts just tweeted that they've won a particularly big contract? Pick up the phone right now and congratulate them. Be part of that moment with them.

- ✔ A contact has just shared a LinkedIn profile update about their new role in a new organisation? Call them today and say how pleased you are and how well they're going to do. Boost their confidence as they get used to their new title.

- ✔ You spot on Facebook that someone is having a rubbish day? Phone now. Don't delay; say, 'Hi mate, spotted that things not going too well, want to talk it through?'

You see, I do this. I'm ferociously busy these days, but talking to people and actually caring about other people's lives is key to who I am and what I do. I love life's rich tapestry and being in touch with the people I care about.

Talking to people in this way strengthens your relationships beyond measure. What if one of your networking contacts took the time to reach out to you in an hour of need or to celebrate your success? I bet you'd want to look out for them in future.

I take it even further and phone people who I've never met in real life but am connected to on social media. I join up my real life and online networking by making those virtual connections to real people by actually talking to them.

In the early days of my networking career, the only form of social media I used was the 4Networking online forum at `4networking.biz/forum`. If I liked what someone wrote on there, I picked up the phone and introduced myself, just to see how the relationship developed. If I was in discussion with someone and we had differing points of view on a subject, I'd call them and make sure that we both knew and respected that the other was a real person and not just a set of characters on a screen.

People talk, and always have, about whether technology adversely affects 'real-life' relationships. First it was books, then motorised transport, radio, television, the Internet, and now social media. The fears are the same as they've always been. Does this new technology mean that people no longer need real-life relationships.

I believe that by blurring the distinction ourselves and by turning those virtual relationships into real-life relationships, at the same time as keeping our real-life relationships alive virtually, that one positively enhances the other.

Here are a few ways that you can turn your virtual relationships into real-life relationships, bringing those people closer to your inner circle of contacts:

✔ That guy you banter with on Twitter – go to his profile, then click the link to his website, then phone the number on there and ask to speak to him. Say 'Hi Steve, you know what, it just struck me that we chat all the time but have never actually spoken.' Then see how the conversation goes.

✔ Have a leaf through your LinkedIn contacts. How many of them do you actually know? Grab a handful of the ones you don't and call them. Do a few every day. Doing so will only take you twenty minutes and you've no idea where these conversations may lead. Put it like this: what's the point of them being a LinkedIn contact if you've no real-life connection with them?

✔ Go through your LinkedIn contacts. Grab a few who you don't know at random. Go to the profile page of each and check their Twitter link. Are they more active on Twitter than they are on LinkedIn? Follow them. Engage with them. Strengthen the relationship there.

✔ Someone sent you a connection request on Facebook or LinkedIn? If you don't know them, pick up the phone and talk to them before you accept the request. Find out what you have in common and why they wanted to connect with you.

✔ If you're visiting one of your networking meetings in a town that's new to you (Passporting with 4Networking or visiting a trade show or event), tweet that you're going there and ask whether any of your contacts want to hook up for a coffee and a one-to-one. This use of technology is how I've met lots of people in real life.

✔ If you spot a request on a forum or tweet that you may be able to help with, *do not* only reply virtually. Pick up the phone. If their phone number isn't obvious, Google it. I've done this thousands of times and only rarely have people not responded positively.

✔ If someone regularly retweets or likes/shares your stuff, connect with them. Call them and talk to them. If at all possible, meet them at some point.

Part IV
Turbo-charging Your Networking

Top Five Tips for Keeping in Touch with Your Contacts

- ✔ Go to networking meetings! You get the chance to talk to 15, 20 or more of your contacts all in a two- or three-hour slot.

- ✔ Keep using social media. You can be there all the time.

- ✔ Attend trade and business shows. Again, you've a huge opportunity here to meet lots of people in a short time frame.

- ✔ Just pick up the phone and give a new contact a call.

- ✔ Dedicate and mark out in your diary a specific time period every week just for talking to people.

Go to www.dummies.com/extras/busines networking for free online bonus content about making the most of business networking.

In this part . . .

✓ Boost your business with personal branding.

✓ Invite others to networking meetings and find other ways to expand your network.

✓ Know the best methods for keeping in touch with people.

✓ Get creative with bartering for services.

✓ Effortlessly make networking a part of your business routine.

Chapter 16

Using Networking to Build Your Business

*N*etworking is more than just being out there and getting your pitch, conversations, one-to-ones and follow up right. Networking is more than just sales for your business.

In this chapter, I discuss what else networking is and how else you can use networking to grow your business. Think about really picking apart your networking activity and using it as more than a marketing tool.

Standing Out in Networking

Networking is something you need to work at and work at constantly. Just pitching up when you have something to sell just won't work.

Being part of the networking scene, constantly assembling and maintaining your crowd, is one of the things that can set you apart from the people who 'dip in and out' of networking depending on when they need the business.

The people who stick out in networking are the ones who are constantly there, in contact with other people, looking out for opportunities for the people around them and impossible to ignore because they're everywhere. I was, and still am, that person.

Putting in the effort

The people who stick out in networking do so because they put in the effort that other people don't want to.

To illustrate the point, consider these recent encounters:

- ✔ When I started talking about the fact that I'd been invited to write this book, people asked me how I'd done it; how I'd got in front of the people from *For Dummies*. The honest answer was that I'd attended over 600 networking meetings in a five-year period, been to every trade and business show I could reasonably get to, built up a pro-file on Twitter, Facebook, LinkedIn, Google+, Instagram, 4Networking and anywhere else where there were people who wanted to talk to me. I'd travelled all over the coun-try talking about networking, even when my nerves got the better of me and I didn't want to be there. And I did all of this networking consistently for five years until I met a commissioning editor for the *For Dummies* series at the Business StartUp Show in London.

  Someone at a networking meeting asked me how they could get in touch with the guys from *For Dummies* because they were also interested in writing a book. I told them that they were in luck because the *For Dummies* people would be at the Business Show in London that very month. This person *really* wants to write a *For Dummies* book. But London, it seems, is just too far for them to travel and, they wonder, would an email suffice instead?

- ✔ I used to run mini-seminars on networking skills. Someone asked me how I got people to attend as they wanted to run seminars themselves. I told them I went to every net-working meeting I could and built a reputation for being someone who was always out there. I did this for a couple of years. I made friends with other influential networkers from around the country and looked out for opportunities for them. I embraced social media as it started to appear in the UK in around 2008 and taught myself how to use it. I did this for a couple of years and *then* I developed my seminars and people wanted to come. They signed up because I'd put in the work to make sure that they knew who I was and wanted to hear what I had to say.

And when I gave that answer, the person who'd asked me looked back and asked what section of the 4Networking website they should advertise on.

Remembering that networking isn't easy

Here's the thing (possibly a dangerous, but honest, thing to put out there). Networking isn't an easy hit. Sure, you can pick up some leads and referrals, particularly if other people in your networking group are obliged to give them to you. You may even pick up a few easy sales just by being out there when you've got something to sell. But the real business, the real value in networking, comes when you really put the effort in and really ensure that you provide lots of value, lots, before you ever expect to see any value back.

One issue that arises in relation to how many people network, and indeed do business, is that they expect the value to come back from the same people they gave value to. It doesn't always work like that. You may give five referrals to one contact and get nothing back from her. She's not a bad person; she's just focused on her business rather than looking for referrals for you. But don't stop. Make sure that you keep giving her referrals because you're solving a problem for every single person you refer to her and, if her service is brilliant (which it must be if you're consistently referring to her), then you're building your credibility with the people you're referring to as well as with her.

You're also building your credibility as a networker with everyone who's watching how you work and noticing how much you look out for opportunities for the other guy (or gal). The more you choose to put yourself out there in networking circles, the more you add value to the lives and businesses of the other people around you, and the more it will come back to you.

Engaging your brain and engaging your network

Let me give you an example of two search engine optimisation (SEO) companies and how they each approached networking.

One advertised on various networking sites and its representative even did a bit of networking himself. He talked about how his services worked and how he was generally less expensive than some of the other companies out there.

The representative from the other company posted on various networking sites offering free advice to anyone who wanted him to look at their site. Someone putting their site up for scrutiny would, after a few days, receive advice in the form of an email plus a personalised video explaining in really simple terms what they should do both within the site and with the external content in order to develop its profile on Google. The same guy also posted lots of general advice on networking sites and wrote a 20,000-word e-book describing what people need to know to do everything that he does.

Guy number one picked up some business. Guy number two, over a period of a few years built himself a marvellous reputation and became the 'go to' guy for SEO advice throughout various communities. Guess what? Many of the people who approached him, even though he'd told them how to do the stuff themselves, preferred him to do it for a fee – *and* he charged what he wanted as they were approaching him and they could already see the value in what he was doing.

Now let me tell you about two human resources (HR) professionals.

One turned up to networking meetings and presented her 40-second introduction perfectly. It was engaging and well-written.

The other delivered an equally good introduction. As well as attending the networking meetings, however, she also socialised with the people around her. She became actively involved in a number of online business communities and, whenever anyone had an off-the-cuff query about HR or employment law matters, she spent a few minutes giving her educated opinion. I even saw her thanked online for spending time on the phone giving people free advice where needed.

The first HR professional picked up a few leads and decided that networking didn't work for HR professionals and gave up. The other developed a regular and valuable stream of referrals from people who she'd connected with and from others who'd simply seen the way she conducted herself in the networking world.

Both of the successful networkers took time to really engage with their crowds, building up a reputation online and in real life, rarely selling but creating the conditions where, as soon as conditions were right, people would buy from them.

I know both the SEO and HR professionals personally and know that they both now have expanding and successful businesses. They did what other people weren't prepared to do – they went the extra mile; they did whatever it took to stand out in a crowded marketplace.

A lot of what you do in networking has an extremely long shelf life and you never know when someone who has been impressed with your work will be in a position to refer to you.

As well as going the extra mile, you have to be there when the time comes that people need or want your services. As well as impressing people, you have to be visible when you've impressed them enough to recommend or refer you.

Do more than anyone else is prepared to do. This business is yours. Do whatever it takes.

Don't disappear just when you've built your reputation and profile.

Finding better ways to advertise than shouting to strangers

If someone walked into a pub and immediately starting shouting at everyone to buy whatever they were selling that would be weird, right?

Assembling a crowd the Google way

Do you look at how some of the bigger brands and businesses behave and the techniques they use to promote themselves and build a crowd or stand out?

I do, every day. You can come across lessons all the time if you look for them and, while you may not have the budget of some of the huge brands (I certainly don't), the basic principles can often be used for free, when you understand what they are. You see, Google understand this, and always has done.

What do you think of first when you think of Google? Do you immediately think of Google Apps – their paid-for office suite and cloud-based storage? No?

Or maybe AdSense, where they pay you a commission to place banner ads on your website? No?

Oh! You think Google AdWords, where they charge you to appear at the top of everyone's search? No?

I'm playing with you, of course.

You thought first of Google as a search engine; when you 'Google' something you need to find. (By the way, if you can build your brand so that it becomes a universally recognised verb, you're doing something *very* right.)

So, with a company that made a profit of over $10.5 *billion* last year, the first thing you thought of was the thing they give away for free *and* gave away for free before they introduced the bits people pay for?

Maybe you want to be as big as Google. I doubt it, though. I'm guessing you want a business that provides the lifestyle you want and is also something you can be proud of.

No matter what size you want to be, you can't deny that the approaches I'm talking about here are exactly those used by Google to assemble its crowd in the first place.

Give away something for free, whether that's advice, content, e-books or free seminars. Make sure that the thing you give away for free is ridiculously good value.

I'm constantly pushing content out there – loads of content about networking, mainly from my blog (noredbraces.co.uk) but also through Twitter, LinkedIn, Tumblr and Medium. Yet people still want to buy my book and pay me to speak.

They know, from what I do, that I give value. I can show that all day long. Google gives stupid value to the people who don't pay. As a paid-up user of several of its services, I can also tell you that the company provides as much value when you do business with it.

Learn from Google. Show people just how much value you can give them. Focus on giving them value upfront, rather than thinking of it as a means to an end.

I'm not sure which is weirder actually, shouting at a completely empty room, or shouting at a bunch of people you don't already know.

But people walk into a networking room, whether in real life or virtually, and the first thing they do is shout to people about what they're selling. You can find a much better way to do it.

Build your crowd first. Give away the stuff for free. Spend time talking to people, looking for opportunities and engaging with your crowd.

When you've done that and when you really do have something to advertise – do it and the people you've given value to want to help and support you.

If you've kept records of the people you've given advice or information to, ask them if they know anyone who your latest offer may be of interest to.

If you keep an email list and regularly send content to people, an occasional ad will get the response you're looking for. If you blog or tweet or share content on Facebook, LinkedIn and Google+, then occasionally sharing some of your own 'buy my stuff' will be well regarded by people.

When people only ever shout about their stuff, they rapidly become boring. If you only appear interested in what you have to sell, other people quickly lose interest in you.

Boosting Your Business with Personal Branding

Personal branding is a hot topic.

Personal branding is the business strategy whereby you consider yourself a brand. You think about what that means in terms of how Brand You acts, identify your strengths and weaknesses, and then market yourself accordingly. Personal branding can be as important for the employed as it is for the business owner or the self-employed.

Personal branding has a lot to do with knowing who you are and what you stand for. If you're passionate about your business and truly believe in it, you're half way to getting this personal branding right. That passion and belief shines through and people feel it as well as hear it.

It also has to do with what you say and how you say it. What you wear and how you present yourself also have some bearing on it.

But, more than anything, what you *do* is what counts.

Learning from Evian's posh bottles

If you've seen any of my 'official' photos, you may have noticed that I'm carrying an Evian bottle. Ever wondered why? I reckon what Evian has to do to get noticed and what we have to do is surprisingly similar.

You see, Evian has a problem. I realised that when I walked into a garage and looked at the cold drinks display in front of me.

There was Evian at £1.19 a bottle, sitting alongside other brands, such as Buxton and Volvic, which were cheaper. These bottled waters provide the same basic combination of hydrogen and oxygen atoms with the odd trace mineral (I did A level chemistry and sometimes like to show off).

So Evian has a problem – it needs us to decide to buy its bottle, even though it's more expensive. The way the company attacks this problem really interests me.

Evian doesn't have a salesperson standing next to the fridge pointing out the features and benefits of its brand of water, nor does it provide a brochure for you to read prior to making a decision. Evian has just seconds to have an impact on you before you work out that what's in that bottle is actually more expensive than what you just filled your car up with.

So it goes for visual impact and makes its product attractive to you, quite subtly and cleverly.

Sorting out your shop front

When I was an estate agent, no matter where I worked, the offices always had something in common.

The shop front of our office was specifically designed to help build our brand and to help people immediately understand what we stood for.

The window display of the last estate agency I worked for was made up of A3 posters for each property, rather than the A4 size used by most estate agents locally. The photographs on our posters had all been taken by professional photographers, rather than on our office camera. The pillars that held the posters in place were oak, rather than the plastic or wire used by most estate agents (alright, they were MDF with a veneer, but they looked the part). The window had particularly subtle uplighters so the display just oozed quality, which was appropriate because we wanted to, and did, attract the sellers of quality properties. We had a reputation for selling the unusual and impressive stuff locally and used our window display to demonstrate that.

I know an estate agency in London that operates an internal rule whereby no paperwork or office detritus is allowed on the desks when the office is shut. Even during the day, the only paperwork allowed on any desk is that being worked on at that moment.

Looking in from the outside, that estate agency promotes an image of calm efficiency – utterly in keeping with the brand it advertises.

The estate agency I used to work for and the outfit in London both use their shop front to display some of their brand values.

One of the things I realised when I started going networking is that the only shop front I had now was me. What I did, how I presented myself, was going to be my shop front whether I wanted it to be or not. People were going to be making judgements about me based on that shop front, based on that Evian bottle – I didn't get to choose whether they judged me, but I did get to choose what they saw.

Evian tints its bottles blue, because when you see blue water you're unconsciously reminded of cool streams, and the sort of clear mountain water you've seen in films. It puts mountain decals around the top of the bottle, further reinforcing the notion that the water is bottled by shepherds high up in a mountain somewhere. It puts a photo of an attractive young person wearing casual and fashionable clothes on the front because, of course, drinking Evian's water makes you healthier and most likely more attractive to the opposite sex. In a final flourish, Evian makes the specially designed 'sports cap' bright red, making certain that that cap, and not the other bottles, is the first thing you notice in the fridge.

So how is this relevant to us, when we get up in the morning and decide to go out networking? Well, we have exactly the same problem. And yet we don't have Evian's massive marketing budget.

We have to be noticed for all the right reasons. Everything we do when we go networking is putting a wrapper around us and becomes our Evian bottle, whether we want it to or not.

People notice much more than we think and people *do* make snap judgements, as much as we advise them not to in networking circles. Know this fact and use it to your advantage.

Identify what you want people to think of you and make sure that you are that person. If you're a personal assistant, how do you want to be perceived? As punctual, organised and efficient? Make sure that is what you actually are. What about a presentation skills coach? You'd better make sure that your introduction is the best in the room. Are you an expert on sales and marketing? Practise what you preach; don't be scared to follow up and close.

I've seen the most convincing presentations ruined by people not being the person that they talked about and I've seen people's presentations being greatly enhanced when they match up to their own description.

Being a product of the product

When you're networking, you have to be a product of the product. You have to be what you do. Doing so is how you decorate your shop front and make sure that your Evian bottle looks exactly how you want it to look.

Remember that what you *do* is at least as important as what you *say*.

A while ago I was at a networking meeting and someone arrived late. What I found interesting was that his lateness wasn't a surprise to the local team; apparently this person was late almost every week. They told me there'd be a 'story', that something would have happened which meant this guy was late.

Sure enough, when he did arrive, 15 minutes after the start of the meeting, he delivered a lengthy explanation about sleeping through his alarm, then missing the bus, then being unable to get on the next bus because it was full, and so on.

As a finale, he then announced that he didn't have enough cash to pay for attendance at the meeting and he'd also forgotten to bring his business cards.

When he was finally settled in, the meeting resumed. Eventually, in the appointed slot, this man stood up and introduced himself as a 'virtual assistant who can take over all the jobs you don't want to do in your business, organise your diary and make sure your To Do list is always done'.

To whom do you want to give the jobs in your business? The guy who can't get up in time to catch the bus and forgot to bring business cards to a business meeting?

This story illustrates how *not* to be a product of the product. This guy was pretty much the exact opposite. What he said in his 40-second introduction was actually pretty good, but you couldn't help but notice that what he said and what he did were two entirely different things.

Here are a few tips for living as a product of the product:

- ✔ If you're going to present yourself as a business or life coach – you have to live it and be the most confident and together person in the room.

- ✔ If you're a PA or virtual assistant, then what I want to see when I look at you is cool, calm organisation.

- ✔ If you design websites, then when I check your website out after the meeting it had better be bloody good. If I check it out and it isn't completed, you've lost my interest.

✔ If you're a social media expert, I should be able to find a credible presence for you all over the place and you should be more up to date on new social media channels than me.

✔ If you can help me get rich and your business cards say 'Printed free by XYZ Print' on the back, then I'm going to smell a rat.

The list goes on for each and every profession and business. I've seen badly dressed image consultants and presentation skills experts who hardly knew how to string a few words together. Equally I've seen many people who consistently and convincingly show off their business through their actions and behaviour when they're networking, both in real life and online.

Work out what you stand for and what your business is about. Live it and make sure that people can see you living it.

Using Networking as an Excuse

So here's some creative thinking. Rather than just pitching up and seeing who you meet at networking events, how about putting thought into who you *want* to see there and making that happen.

I consistently used my networking groups as an excuse for making contact with people. It may not be the most elegant way of selling, but it was extremely useful in getting me in front of the people I wanted to meet.

Getting to your ideal prospects using networking

The first thing you need to do is try to find out whether your ideal prospect goes to networking events themselves.

A small team I wanted to work with did. They'd tweet about it and I'd engage with them and talk about the networking events we both went to.

I was based in Oxfordshire, they in Hertfordshire, but I really wanted to work with them, so booked myself into a meeting that I knew they were going to be at and managed to have a one-to-one with them to get to know them better. They became clients of mine and, as it happens, I became a client of theirs too.

That was simple; it just took some effort and planning on my part, and a willingness to get up and drive two hours for the right opportunity.

But what if you've done your research and your ideal prospect doesn't go networking?

Invite them.

Simple; if you really want to meet someone, you have a couple of choices. You can pick up the phone, tell them what you do and why you're interested in talking to them and see whether they can spare half an hour to talk to you. Now you may be a brilliant cold caller; you may be the best in the world. But I bet that approach doesn't always work for you.

How about picking up the phone and saying that you're a member of a business club that meets every couple of weeks in this hotel with the intention of passing business around local members, and would they fancy coming along and seeing what the club is about? If true, you can say you're approaching them because you don't currently have an estate agent/accountant/solicitor or whatever it happens to be as a member.

Presuming they choose to come along, and many people will, you then have a connection. More than a connection, you're in prime position to greet them when they do arrive, introduce yourself again and make sure that you get one of the first one-to-ones with them. You can now have a ten-minute conversation and start to develop that relationship with your ideal prospect.

I know people who use this approach specifically to build their business. Particularly, I know people who are aware that their business is a difficult 'sell' or that what they do can't be sold on the first meeting, so inviting someone along to a networking meeting gives them the opportunity to build the relationship over time.

If your networking group is a credible one, then the prospect will even be grateful to you for bringing them along. They may even meet people who are interested in their services, and you'll be the person who invited them.

Using networking for businesses that can't cold call

Some businesses *can't* cold call. Financial advisers, for example, are so regulated in the UK these days that they can't call people out of the blue and talk about a lot of what they do.

So why not invite the people you want to do business with to your networking meeting? You *can* call other businesses and invite them along and you *can* then talk to them about what you do, after, of course, you've talked about what they do too.

Again, I know many independent financial advisors (IFAs) who use networking meetings in just this kind of way, in order to build their business and constantly expand their contacts, their prospects and their clients.

Instead of just waiting to see who pitches up, you can, if you choose to, take some control over who comes to your next networking meeting.

This initiative is, again, something that most people won't do. You can greatly improve your results from networking by taking the effort to do so.

Write down a list of the people and businesses you've long wanted to speak to. Get contact details, then call them and invite them and make sure that you're there to greet them, grab them a coffee and get a one-to-one with them.

Chapter 17

Building Networking into Your Business Strategy

In This Chapter

▶ Integrating networking into your business

▶ Keeping in constant touch with your contacts

▶ Learning from the little things that the big winners do

*H*ave you ever wondered why some people consistently get fantastic results from networking and others achieve only sporadic success?

Over the last six years or so I've observed how some people seamlessly integrate networking into their business. Networking isn't something they do, but something they live and their business benefits as a result.

Someone once said that 'networking is more an attitude than an activity' and in this chapter I show you how to develop that attitude and the activities to make it work.

Circles Within Circles: It Isn't Just About Who You Know

People often describe networking, and business in general, as being about who you know. The more people you know, the more links you have in your networking chain and the closer you get to your ideal contact.

Your contacts resemble circles within circles; with some you have a really strong connection and with others a much looser relationship.

As much as being about who you know, networking is about who knows you. If you're already involved in networking organisations, who are the people everyone else talks about?

> 'Have you met Sanjay – he knows everyone who's anyone?'

> 'Talk to Mary, she's been a member for at least five years and gets *loads* of business as a result.'

These kinds of people are the ones you want to emulate – to watch how they approach networking and copy as much of it as you can. I bet they're doing a fair number of the following things:

- ✔ Attending networking events regularly and consistently
- ✔ Presenting the ten-minute slot often and at different groups
- ✔ Getting involved in online networking and social media
- ✔ Being part of the local team organising the networking meetings
- ✔ Constantly looking for and providing opportunities for others
- ✔ Being a friendly, cheerful and helpful part of any networking meetings they're at so that people *want* to know them

To make sure that people talk about you in a positive light, try these tips:

- ✔ Make sure that any work you do for a member of your networking group is spectacular so that they talk about you.
- ✔ Try to work with some of the opinion formers and people who are already well known in your local networking circles.
- ✔ Work on your 40-second and 10-minute presentations to make them memorable. Doing so will help people talk about them later.

✔ Follow up with everyone. Your remembering them helps them to remember you.

✔ Attend any social events your networking group organises. You don't have to be the life and soul of every party but being there and allowing relationships to flourish out of business uniform will accelerate your success.

As you get to know loads of people make sure that even more people get to know you. Be recognised by the quality of your work, your attitude to networking and your overall reputation.

Networking provides so many opportunities to get yourself out there and known – locally, regionally, nationally or even internationally. So get out and do it!

Staying in Touch When You Said You Would

Never make empty promises. Keeping in touch with everyone takes effort but is certainly worthwhile. Think about sensible and efficient ways to keep in touch with people:

✔ Go to networking meetings. You get the chance to talk to 15, 20 or even more of your contacts in one two- or three-hour slot.

✔ Keep using social media. You can be there all the time.

✔ Attend trade and business shows. They provide the opportunity to meet lots of people within a short time frame.

✔ Pick up the phone.

Dedicate a specific time every week to talking to people – and put it in your diary.

Finding people to talk to

I doubt you'll ever experience a shortage of people to talk to who can potentially expand your network. If you think you've run out of potential contacts, consider these:

✔ **Current clients:** Find out how things are with them. Do they have any questions they've been meaning to ask you? Are you waiting on anything from them?

✔ **Ex-clients:** Check out how their business is going. Ask if they operate an email mailing list and, if they do, whether you can be added to it so that you can keep up to date with developments their end.

✔ **People who've asked for info but not proceeded:** Find out if they're still looking for the service you offered.

✔ **People in your networking meetings:** If you haven't had a conversation with them outside of specific events, now's your chance. Meet up for a coffee and just chat; you may discover lots of interesting things about their business. Make sure you're connected on Facebook, LinkedIn, Google+ or Twitter.

✔ **People in your networking circles who you don't know well:** Try to get to know them better. Connect on social media or identify a networking event that you can both get to in the near future and pre-book a one-to-one.

Keep an up-to-date list of the people you want to know better or to connect with again. I use Evernote for this list and make a few calls whenever I have some down time or just need to do something different for a while.

Talking to people *is* working, particularly if you're running a small business. Engaging with people who might become part of your network, or a more active part of your network than they are, is incredibly useful.

Growing your network as people come and go

People's lives, businesses and circumstances invariably change. If you've spent time building a relationship with someone, losing touch with them if they move to a different organisation or relocate elsewhere makes no sense at all.

LinkedIn is particularly good for keeping you informed of someone's business movements. If they change company or title or responsibilities and update their profile to record this information, LinkedIn posts an update on their timeline alerting you to the change.

Also keep an eye on people's Twitter feeds and Facebook updates for any changes that you can congratulate them on and thus establish contact.

Thinking Outside the Limited Company

Too many people think of networking in terms of 'What can I sell to her?' or, if you're lucky, 'What can I buy from her?' or, if you're really lucky, 'Who can I refer to her?' However, successful people grow their business by also asking 'How can I work with her?'

Your business may be involved in selling one thing, but often, by forming a loose relationship with someone else who offers a complementary service, you can expand your market and reputation.

I've seen several win-win networking setups:

- ✔ A website designer and a copywriter formed a loose relationship and agreed to offer each other's services. Doing so resulted in several benefits.

  A website designer often has to wait for the client's copy. Offering a copywriting service meant that the client's text was written to a professional standard and delivered as soon as possible, the website was then finished sooner, the copywriter won business she wouldn't otherwise have had access to and the website designer was able to sign the project off and invoice quicker. Everyone, including the client, was a winner.

- ✔ Several financial advisers with differing specialities organised a number of mini-seminars to explain different aspects of financial planning. Each advisor invited all of his clients. Again, the setup was successful for all concerned.

  If one adviser's speciality was mortgages but he was able to invite his clients to a free seminar providing pension advice, his clients received worthwhile and relevant extra value. A second benefit was that the clients were kept within the small informal network of financial advisers rather than being lost to other providers. Finally, the event provided an opportunity for each adviser to meet and network with their clients.

✔ Two business coaches using different approaches and styles joined up and offered short courses to their respective clients. As they discovered, two mailing lists are better than one; selling someone else's 'stuff' is sometimes easier than selling your own; and merging their offering gave their respective clients something new to think about.

In each scenario, the end game was to find a different opportunity to talk to existing contacts while simultaneously meeting new contacts.

Some people think that they can't work with others in similar industries because they're in competition. For most service providers, however, there is plenty of business to go round and working with other people is likely to bring you more business. I know many website designers who refer business to each other as they have different specialities and enjoy working on different aspects of the process.

Bartering to build your business

When you're first starting up, ready cash may be an issue. If you can't afford all the things you need for your business, consider bartering with members of your networking groups.

I was able to offer my copywriting service in exchange for business cards, a website, graphic designs for said website and profile photographs.

In return for the work these people did, I offered a proportionate amount of my services in return. Thus, if the photographer provided £250 worth of profile photographs for me, I provided the same amount of copywriting for their new website. The website designer who built my first website then offered my copywriting services to his clients for a charge or as a bonus; he retrieved the value either way.

Obviously you can't just pitch up and ask for people's services for free. You first need to create a reputation and demonstrate the value of your own work. But the opportunity for bartering certainly exists within networking circles.

This practice does, however, come with a warning. You have bills and maybe a mortgage to pay. You may also have little mouths to feed (or maybe just your own big mouth). If someone wants to barter with you, be absolutely sure that they're offering something that you want or need in return. Use bartering with care and make sure that it works equally for both parties.

If you enter a loose partnership or joint venture with someone else, agree on ground rules as soon as possible. Make it clear who's doing what to avoid future frustration or disagreements.

Building Your Virtual Team

Creating a virtual organisation from the people in your networking circles is perfectly possible and can be spectacularly successful.

Finding people you trust along the way can give you the opportunity to take on much bigger projects than previously. You can pull in expertise and labour from other people around you. I've yet to meet a small business working at maximum capacity, so credible people will always be around who'll be happy to work with you.

If you're an expert networker, out there creating opportunities for others, you'll also find opportunities for yourself and be able to create a team around you to take advantage of them. Every service you can think of is represented at networking events and you have the benefit of knowing the people you pull into your virtual team.

Think of the alternative. If you're a self-employed website designer who doesn't go networking and you get the opportunity to work on a huge project with a decent budget – will you be able to do it on your own, or will you have to turn it down?

If you do go networking and always look for people you think you can work with, you can immediately assemble the right people. Not only are you able to say yes to the project, but you also enhance your professional reputation and create opportunities for other people in your networking circles.

Everyone's a winner.

I've watched several small-business owners transform themselves from one-man bands to project managers on large-scale projects using their networking contacts.

Think about how you want to grow your business. Can you work alongside your networking colleagues so that the whole becomes greater than the sum of the parts?

Settling Into a Routine and Knowing What Works for You

In order for networking to work as part of your business, you have to make it part of your business. Dipping in and out of networking doesn't work.

The danger is that you only go networking when you're quiet and have nothing else in your diary. In other words, you only go networking when you've an empty bucket and need the other people in the room to fill it.

Make networking part of your weekly routine. Plan in advance and put your networking meetings in your diary. Use your networking time to simultaneously catch up with the people you do know and introduce yourself to people you don't yet know.

Think about your business and how it works so that you can concentrate on networking when you're networking. Find networking events that fit into your routine and your timescale so that your business is covered when you need it to be. Think about lunch or evening events if breakfasts don't work for you. Whatever you do, make a plan and stick to it.

You derive maximum benefit from networking if you see the same people every week and also meet new people. Aim to do some of each in your networking plan.

If you want networking to work for your business, make networking part of that business and watch what happens.

Part V
Measuring Your Success

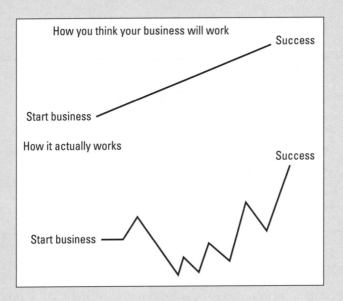

How you think your business will work

Success

Start business

How it actually works

Success

Start business

Go to www.dummies.com/extras/busines networking for free online bonus content about making the most of business networking.

In this part . . .

- ✔ Make notes so you can measure your networking success.
- ✔ Find the hidden value in networking.
- ✔ Know the importance of feedback and solve any networking issues.
- ✔ Test new products or launches with your networking crowd.

Chapter 18

Networking or Notworking?

. . . .

In This Chapter

▶ Working out if your networking is successful

▶ Making notes after every networking meeting

▶ Adopting the right frame of mind for networking

. . . .

So, you've started networking but how do you know whether it's working for you? Come to that, how do you know what 'working' looks like when applied to networking?

In this chapter I look at how (and to some extent whether) to measure the success of your networking activity, along with advice and tips on how to make it more successful.

Measuring your Return on Investment

When you've been engaged in any business activity for a while, you need to measure how successful that activity has been for your business. Continuing to do something that isn't working clearly makes no sense. Equally, you need to recognise if something is working well for your business so that you can continue doing it, or even do more of it.

Many business people also undertake a process of continuous improvement; analysing what they're doing and then tweaking and making small adjustments to it. Networking is no different and understanding what is and isn't working in your approach is vital. Unfortunately, networking may be more difficult to measure.

Ever-helpful Evernote

I'm a big fan of Evernote. Wikipedia describes Evernote as a suite of software and services designed for notetaking and archiving. I describe it as a place to download everything I need to remember.

In simple terms, Evernote enables you to take quick notes that are then synchronised across every device on which you install Evernote. It then allows you to archive, label, tag and organise those notes in any way which works for you. Visit https://evernote.com/ for more information.

Consider the following scenario: you decide to print and distribute 1,000 leaflets for a local marketing campaign. You get two responses, only one of which then signs up for your offering. Your return on investment is simple to measure and easy to calculate. You can also reasonably predict that if you produce 10,000 leaflets, you'll receive around 20 responses. Only you know if that represents the right return on investment for you.

But how do you measure your networking results? You may go to a meeting with 30 people, broadcast your message to all of them and have one-to-one meetings with three. Over time, you may have one-to-ones with all 30 network members. But it may still take time before any of them buy from you.

Which is more successful? The leaflet campaign generating a 0.2 per cent response rate and a customer straight away; or the networking activity providing an immediate 10 per cent response?

Confused already?

Recognising and recording the value in every meeting

Treat every networking meeting as an event in its own right, rather than grouping together several months' worth of networking activity and trying to work out your success then. Analysing each individual event allows you to plot your progress and acknowledge small successes. If you're only looking for big results, by the time you decide to measure your success you may have already decide that networking isn't working for you.

Always record the results of your networking activities. Whichever medium you choose, be it paper, iPad or Evernote, stick with it.

So what sort of information should you record? Consider asking yourself the following questions after every networking event:

- ✔ How many people attended? How many people did I have the opportunity to introduce my business to?

- ✔ How many people did I have one-to-one meetings with, either formally or in the open networking time before and after the meeting?

- ✔ Were these people potential clients?

- ✔ Were any potential referral partners attending? How about businesses whose customers may also benefit from my services?

- ✔ Did I meet any suppliers who could save me money or provide better service than my current supplier?

- ✔ Have I specifically arranged to follow up with anyone? Have I made a note of any actions I promised?

- ✔ Did I get any good feedback on my ten-minute presentation?

- ✔ If I didn't present, did I find out anything new from the ten-minute presentation? How may it be useful to my business? When do I plan to implement it?

- ✔ Did I receive any helpful feedback about my approach? How and when will I implement any changes?

Make notes on as many of your responses as you deem useful.

Finding the hidden value in networking

Often people want to judge their networking results purely on how many sales they've made or referrals they've received. This approach is fatally flawed because it makes much of your networking activity appear and feel unsuccessful. If you leave every networking meeting and event judging its success purely on whether or not you've sold something, more often than not you'll be disappointed.

A better approach is to view networking as a journey and to acknowledge the many other benefits you receive from it:

- ✔ **Social.** Being self-employed can be a lonely experience. Consider the value of regular social events at which you meet up with like-minded people in a similar position.

- ✔ **Supportive.** If you have a problem you can discuss it with members of your networking circle. You can probably find people who've faced the same problem or something similar and can offer advice.

- ✔ **Educational.** Your networking circle gives you the opportunity to try out new ideas and pitches and to perfect your sales presentation in a safe and supportive environment.

- ✔ **Customer research.** Your best idea ever may need refining, you may need to rethink your pricing or how you package your service – networking is the ideal environment in which to conduct research and seek feedback from others around you.

- ✔ **Personal development.** You're likely to get better at public speaking and presenting to other people as part of your networking journey.

- ✔ **Commercial.** You may save money or find better suppliers along the way.

- ✔ **Sales.** And yes, you'll probably sell some of your offering.

Adjusting Your Mindset to Spot the Benefits

Your success as a networker can often hinge on the frame of mind in which you approach networking opportunities. Are you positive and open-minded? You'll probably see some benefits quickly – whether they're the ones you expected or not!

Are you wary and ready to ditch something at the first sign that it appears to be not for you? You're limiting your chance of success before you've even said a word.

Listening to your intuition

In the world of business, and particularly if you're self-employed, you'll always encounter people who know better than you. You know they know better than you because they tell you. While these people have always existed, the advent of social media has created any army of armchair business experts, marketing experts, legal experts and so on. Basically, these are people who like to tell you how much cleverer they are than you.

When you're new in business, you can easily get side-tracked, question your own judgement and not trust your intuition. If people appear to have been around longer than you, or have more business experience, then you can easily start to believe that they *must* know better.

Trust your instincts, not only in relation to networking but across all of your business activities.

People don't like to blame themselves for their own failings so, when someone tells you that this networking group doesn't work, or that by now you should be making sales, or that networking doesn't work for your industry, or that a particular networking group doesn't have the right sort of people, perhaps the real issue is that they can't make it work for themselves.

Self-employment versus business ownership

When I first started networking I was self-employed rather than a business owner. I define these terms as follows:

✔ A business owner has a scalable enterprise, which, although typically run by the owner, doesn't rely on her day-to-day input for the business to continue and grow.

✔ A self-employed person typically does all of the work of the business. She is completely in control and accepts that work will, at best, slow down if she's absent or on holiday.

Some people start by being self-employed and then go on to develop businesses. Others are happy to continue to be self-employed.

Are you enjoying your networking journey? Are you starting to see leads and opportunities coming your way? Measure your success in terms of networking's many benefits, and trust yourself to decide whether you feel that it's working for you.

Keeping an open mind

I recently met someone who'd clearly decided in advance that a particular networking meeting wasn't going to be successful for her. Too few people were in attendance (15-ish), someone else in the room offered a similar offering to her own and she wanted longer than 40 seconds to introduce her business. And she told me all this before the meeting had even started.

Unsurprisingly, she left the networking meeting feeling disappointed and that she'd wasted the three hours she'd taken out of her busy schedule.

I've been involved in many sales environments over the years in which every ounce of effort was put into simply getting in front of people, any people, to talk about our business. Businesses pay thousands of pounds for stands at trade shows, just for the potential opportunity of talking to people about their business.

Yet this woman decided that the opportunity to present her business to 15 other businesses, have one-to-one meetings with some of them, collect business cards, arrange follow ups, listen to an informative presentation by another business owner *and* have a nice lunch (I remember it well, proper chips!) was a waste of time.

In contrast, the person with a similar offering decided to keep an open mind, smile, enjoy the meeting and see what came of it. She left with a prospect to follow up and a smile still on her face.

 Decide that the next networking meeting you go to will be a success. Tell yourself that it doesn't matter who's in the room, how many people are present, what the food's like or how entertaining the ten-minute presentation is. It will be successful for you no matter what.

And remember to smile.

Acknowledging that networking is always working

Even when you may think that networking isn't working for you – for that very reason, it *is* working. If you're not getting sales, you're getting feedback that your approach, your product or your strategy needs adjusting. This change of mindset really helps you get the best from networking.

Often people only judge their networking success based on how many sales they've made but the really successful networkers make sure that they make every meeting successful – whether or not they've won any business.

What isn't working about talking to other people about your business? What isn't working about getting great feedback on whether people want to buy what you're currently selling? What isn't working about meeting with other like-minded business people?

When you treat networking as a continuous journey, that's when it really starts to work for you.

Chapter 19

Revisiting Your Approach

In This Chapter

▶ Figuring out what to do if networking isn't working out

▶ Solving networking issues

▶ Recognising when networking is working even when you think it isn't

*S*o you've put on your best networking smile, delivered a winning introduction, done the ten-minute slot, repeated the process several times and still nothing. Not a bite. Not one person interested in your product or service. Don't give up! In this chapter, I give you some strategies to make your networking efforts a success.

I look at what to do if you think that it isn't working. Some points revisit the obvious and some help you rethink how you're using networking.

Using Networking as a Sounding Board

Some of the biggest value I get from networking is the feedback I receive, both asked for and forced upon me, from the people in my networking circles.

In fact, the opportunity to be with a group of trusted and friendly people to use as a test-bed and sounding board and to get feedback from about what you're doing in a non-'mission critical' environment would be valuable on its own, without all the other benefits that networking brings.

I work alongside people who are good enough to tell me if I'm barking up the wrong tree, or simply getting something 'wrong'. These are people I've met through networking and have known a number of years now. Having that close relationship with them, I trust that they're telling me for the right reasons, usually to stop me making a fool of myself –again.

But if you don't have those relationships yet, how do you get feedback in the early days? Well, often the feedback is there, you just have to listen hard for it. Often, more often than most people spot, the feedback really is all around you. In order to get the best value from networking, learn to listen for it and, most importantly, act on it. Recognising minor improvements you can make, and then taking action to improve, sets you head and shoulders above most people.

The following sections describe several types of silent feedback and actions you can take.

Nobody's asking you for a one-to-one

You turn up, deliver your 40 seconds and yet nobody ever asks you for a one-to-one. When the group leader asks who doesn't have a one-to-one set up, your hand is the one that goes up and you always end up having one-to-ones with people you had a one-to-one with last week, when nobody asked you either.

Nobody has told you your 40 seconds is 'bad'. In fact, people even laugh along with the joke you put in there every week. But still nobody is asking you for a one-to-one.

Plenty of people just plough on and then bemoan the fact that the 'wrong' people are in the networking group and nobody understands what they're offering anyway. But if you want to move your business forward and take the real value from networking, spend a little time analysing what can be done to improve your results.

 Immediately ask yourself, 'Where is my business coming from?' and 'Am I currently getting enough business?'

If you have a list of marketing activities that are working for you and you're getting enough business, then the fact that nobody is asking you for a one-to-one is incredibly useful feedback. If that's the case, here's what you do:

1. **Establish whether your offering is 'packaged' correctly for this networking environment.**

   You don't have to change what you're doing, just how you offer it to your networking contacts. The likelihood is that right now, they don't completely understand what you're doing and how your offering is priced.

2. **Have a look at your other marketing material and establish which bits of that work.**

3. **Revisit your 40-second introduction and make sure that you have solid and clear 'soundbites' as well as the correct call to action for the networking environment.**

   Read Chapter 8 and then work on a few new introductions.

4. **Change your introduction.**

   Did your new introduction work? If it did, great; if it didn't, change it again. Repeat until you get it right and people are queuing up for a one-to-one with you.

Business is dribbling in

What if, actually, you aren't getting enough business; the work is dribbling in but you don't know where it's coming from, from one week to the next. People not asking you for a one-to-one is the most valuable bit of feedback you're ever going to get – ever.

You may not want to accept it straightaway, but what you're offering isn't what people want to buy. You can try to sell stuff that people don't want or need, but you have to be a heck of a salesperson and have a great complaints department too.

When I first started going networking, I was selling something that people didn't want to buy. I could have flogged that horse for months and still nothing would've happened. But it wasn't all bad news. Without getting it wrong at first, I would never have discovered how to get it right. You've already invested in the relationships, as well as the business cards and website, so now is the time to dig in and make this thing work.

Here's what to do:

1. **Contact someone you trust.**

2. **Ask him if he's able to spend a couple of hours with you working on your business introduction.**

3. **Get together with a load of blank paper, ideally A3 or flip-chart size, and pens.**

4. **Provide coffee and biscuits.**

5. **Write down what you do, what is working, what you love doing, what you hate doing, what other people who are doing similar things to you are doing, what your pricing is, what your competitors' pricing is.**

6. **Ask your buddy to be brutally honest as you pick apart what you do, then piece it back together based on what you've written.**

7. **Make sure that what you love doing is a big feature of what you offer.**

8. **Package your introduction differently; write a new 40 seconds using different words to describe what you do.**

   Use Chapter 8 to ensure your 40 seconds is structured correctly.

9. **Go out there and try it.**

   Has that worked? Have you got a queue of people?

10. **Meet up again with your buddy and change your introduction if necessary.**

11. **Repeat these steps until it does work.**

Do these steps sound like hard work to you? I'm sorry if they do but few people get their intro perfect first time round. I hate to break it you but few people get it perfect even second time round. For most successful businesses, their success is the result of constant tweaking and improvement.

You're getting one-to-ones but nobody's buying

You deliver a brilliant 40 seconds, people ask you for a one-to-one but that's where it ends. Well, relax, because this situation is horribly common and equally easy to fix.

Tell me how your follow up works. When you've had a one-to-one with someone and you honestly believe they may be interested in what you do *and* you think that talking to them further may be beneficial, what do you do? Do you get your diary out at the end of the one-to-one and book something else up? No, okay. Do you connect on LinkedIn straight away and then call and ask if you can have a coffee? You don't? Do you send them a postcard, plus call to follow up and explain why you think that meeting up for half an hour would be sensible? You don't do that either, fair enough.

Opportunity does knock – but you must open the door and let it in!

You don't have to sell. You have plenty of opportunity to get to know people and build the relationship. But you're the one lucky enough to have read this book, so take some responsibility for driving the relationship rather than letting it meander.

Have you ever had great one-to-ones with someone and then felt your heart sink a couple of months later when they buy the same service that you offer from someone else? Maybe the other person was more proactive than you.

Do something about it. Make following up part of your networking, not an afterthought. Check out Chapter 11 for ideas on how to follow up effectively.

You view knock backs negatively

You need to change your attitude to negative feedback. If your offering is greeted with absolute silence, you're *really* lucky because the feedback couldn't be clearer.

Often, someone's success in business and networking can be measured by whether they listened for that feedback, took personal responsibility for it and actually made the necessary changes, or whether they ploughed on regardless, blaming everyone else for their failings.

For many people, success in business and networking isn't what they expected it to be; it looks a little more like the graph in Figure 19-1.

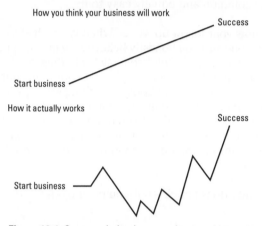

How you think your business will work

Success

Start business

How it actually works

Success

Start business

Figure 19-1: Success in business and networking may not be what you expect!

Knockbacks help to form and shape your offering and your packaging and your presentation. It's those knockbacks that give you the light-bulb moments to move what you're doing forward.

Take complete responsibility for moving your business forward and for what you achieve in your networking and the knockbacks won't hurt so much because you simply see them as part of the process of moving you forward.

Using Your Networking Contacts to Advise You

As well as listening for feedback, don't be shy about asking other people for it, particularly as you get to know and trust them.

When you have a one-to-one with someone, ask them what they thought of your 40 seconds and whether they have any feedback for you. Ask them if, based on your introduction, they can identify what you do.

When you do the ten-minute speaker slot, ask a couple of people, before you start and privately, to give you feedback afterwards. If a presentation skills trainer, or similar, is in the room, ask them for feedback too.

Early on in my speaking career, I was lucky enough to present a ten-minute session at a networking event attended by a business coach, Charles Macadam.. Immediately after my presentation, he kindly took the time to explain that my body language was demonstrating my nervousness to the audience. That little chat, which he probably doesn't even remember, was a turning point in what I was doing. I read *Body Language For Dummies,* 2nd Edition, by Elizabeth Kuhnke (Wiley) and actively set about improving my presentation skills.

I've given people advice and they've told me I'm wrong and carried on as before. Some people will read this book and do the same. I've done that, too. I don't blame them at all. But if you can, rise above it, swallow your pride, take advice from the people around you and make those little changes.

Launching new products to your networking crowd

Have you got a brilliant idea that can take your business forward?

You have a captive audience of known and trusted friends and associates in your networking circles. Use those networks to try out new ideas on and then refine your ideas in the light of their feedback before you take them to the public and market them hard.

I see many 'soft' launches of new ideas and products at networking meetings. People's response to your idea or product when you first introduce it is an incredibly valuable source of research. And if they take it up, even better!

Use your networking contacts to help you refine and define your offering. I offer discounts to 'early adopters' at networking events in the hope that they'll give me valuable feedback before I take my offering to market. I'm honest about its current imperfections and they're generally helpful in return.

Make something 'good enough' and get it out there rather than spend longer making it perfect. Your networking circles are an ideal, and safe, environment in which to launch new stuff.

Trying new pitches

I regularly change my 40-second introduction at 4Networking. Doing so gives me the opportunity to try out new ideas and new ways of describing what I do.

In real life, if I want to try out a new pitch I have to cold-call a potential client. The conversation may go something like this:

> 'Hi Steve, thanks for taking my call. I'm Stefan from No Red Braces and I help businesses build hype and reputation, making sure that as many people as possible know about you and what you do. I'm wondering if you and I could meet for coffee next week so that I can tell you a little more about it.'

> 'Thanks Stefan, but we're really not interested right now.'

> 'Okay Steve, here's the thing. I know that pitch didn't work on you and respect your decision not to take it forward but I must tell you that I've got some much better pitches. Honestly, I've got an absolutely brilliant one I'd like to try out on you tomorrow morning. How about I call back then and try a different pitch and see if you react to that? And you know what, even if that doesn't work, I've got loads more so will call back every day to find the one that does get you interested. Is that okay with you?'

I have no idea how to spell the sound of a phone being put down, so won't even try!

In networking, however, if my 40-second introduction doesn't work this morning, I can come back next week and try something different and, get this, *nobody will mind.*

In real life, when you pitch to someone and they say no, you can hardly ever go back and try again. In networking, you can keep refining and changing until your pitch does work. Don't just plough on regardless; listen to the feedback and then try something new.

Relax – getting it wrong doesn't matter

Stop worrying about making mistakes. The more you stress about it, the more you convey your anxiety to the people around you. Ultimately, if you commit to networking being part of your business plan, then your success or failure at one single networking meeting doesn't matter, because your overall plan is based on networking over a period of time, not just at one meeting.

Tailoring your approach to your environment

It may be that what worked for you at BNI doesn't work in 4N, or vice versa. Or the approach that's stood you in great stead in your local networking group is ineffective now you're with a larger joined-up network.

This problem isn't the network's fault! Each network has a different structure, character and way of doing things. Asking for referrals in a referral-based organisation is what's expected. Asking for them in a networking environment may fall on deaf ears.

 If your business and your offering is sound, make subtle changes to how you package it and how you approach different networking environments. Practise and refine and practise again until your pitch is right for each one.

Discovering the secret to turning around your networking experience

The big secret is that one mistake doesn't matter; one meeting where you mess up your introduction doesn't matter.

 Networking is a safe environment. You can do stuff in networking that you can never do in real life. You can build relationships in your networking circles that give you the opportunity to try things and make mistakes along the way.

It took me far too long to discover this secret but I always keep it in mind now. Everyone else worries about their stuff much more than they worry about yours. Remember that little mistake you made that still haunts you; that business idea you tried that didn't work out? Everyone else has forgotten about it because they're focusing on their own problems.

Often people don't try anything new because they're frightened of failing. Lots of books are written on this very subject. The realisation that nobody else actually cares that much when you fail can be a huge eye opener.

They're not selfish people, but stuff just happens and then life moves on. Do you ever think about the man whose jokes fell flat or the woman who couldn't actually define what her product did? Of course you don't. Those presentations weren't important to you the second they finished.

Pick yourself up, dust yourself down and then deliver presentations that *do* make people sit up and pay attention.

Keeping Faith with Networking

Your network grows over time. As it grows, not only do you make connections with new people but you also lose contact with others. Some people simply drift away; other people's businesses get so big that they run out of time for networking. Some fail and have to return to paid employment. Some people get old and retire; others get sick and die.

Networking circles are constantly changing. You may think that stopping networking is fine because you know all these people already and don't need to see them over breakfast once a fortnight. However, your network will begin to shrink as people leave and you don't invite new people into your circles.

Your contacts may continue networking and meet other people who provide the same offering as you. Clearly, they now start to form a relationship with them.

As well as avoiding shrinking your contact base, maintaining your relationship with your networking groups benefits your reputation and profile. People like stability, plus your long-term commitment to your networking groups makes you seem reliable and trustworthy.

Anyone who goes networking is used to those people who dip in and out. The consistent long-game players, the people who have had successes and failures and kept going whatever, tend to win out. These people are the ones who build up the best relationships and achieve the greatest commercial success from networking.

The more time I spend with someone, the more I get to know about them – their background, skillset, sense of humour, that thing they also do but don't publicise – all of the stuff that makes it easier for me to find opportunities for them in future.

Don't think that you can drop networking for a couple of years and then pick up again where you left off. When you come back, you'll find a whole new crowd of people and new relationships and you'll have to start again from scratch. Turnover is an inevitable aspect of networking and, if you become part of that turnover, you have to let everyone get used to you again.

Getting a second chance to make a first impression

I fell in love with networking from the outset. I worked in several different sales environments over the years and lost count of how many times I was told that old business and sales maxim that you only get one chance to make a first impression.

Well, I've attended over 620 4Networking meetings in the last six years. These meetings are the only environment in which I've been given a second chance, and even a 622nd chance, to make a first impression.

Every new networking meeting is a potential first impression for you. Grab that opportunity.

Part VI

The Part of Tens

Go to www.dummies.com/extras/busines networking for free online bonus content about making the most of business networking, including a bonus Part of Tens chapter.

In this part . . .

- ✔ Take your networking to the next level by running seminars and attending new groups.

- ✔ Identify and avoid common business networking pitfalls.

Chapter 20

Ten Ways to Improve Your Networking Results

*N*etworking isn't going quite as you want? Don't worry. In this chapter, I offer you ten quick tips to get better results from your networking efforts.

Do More Networking

Often, when people tell me they aren't getting anything from networking, they simply aren't doing enough of it or haven't been doing it for long enough.

Go to more networking events, connect and engage with more people on social media, talk to people in your networking circles more often.

And be patient – networking is a long game. Many people give up just before they're about to have a big breakthrough, like swimming the Channel and turning back when sight of land is actually just over the horizon.

Become Part of Your Group's Team

Probably the easiest way to raise your profile in networking circles is to become part of the team running the local group or groups. You become a figurehead, have an excuse to call anyone you like and create the opportunity to grow and develop your own skills.

Often, people tell me they don't have time to become part of the team. See it for the opportunity it is. View the time you're using to develop your local networking group as part of your own marketing activity.

Volunteer for the Ten-Minute Slot

You don't remember every introduction given by every person in the room, even in a small group. But you do remember the person who did the ten-minute slot that morning.

Put together a presentation that gives real value to the other people in the room. Give away tips or information that they can use in their business if they want to. Establish your position as an expert in what you do.

Take an Honest Look at Your 40-Second Introduction

Ask a few close contacts if your 40 seconds makes sense to them. Immediately after you deliver a presentation ask the people to the left and right of you what they really thought of it. Go away and rework your introduction and then try it again. Refine your words and delivery until you receive a response from your audience that satisfies you.

Networking meetings are a fantastic place to get feedback – feedback that you ask for or observe. Use it.

Attend Meetings of Other Networking Groups

Keep refreshing and growing your network by adding new people to it. If your networking organisation allows it, go along and check out other networking groups. You never know who may know somebody who needs your service, may be looking for someone to partner with or knows the contact you've been desperate to get an 'in' with. Push your boundaries a little and get out there.

A consequence of widening your contacts in this way is that you also become popular in your local group as people recognise how wide and valuable your network is.

Phone People

Pick up the phone to some of your networking contacts. Start with the people you've never had a one-to-one with and arrange them for the next networking meeting. Talk to people you know from social media but have never met in real life. Find something about them or their business that interests you and talk to them about it. Don't have an agenda in mind; just see where the conversation goes.

Run a Mini-Seminar after a Networking Event

This section is straight from the heart as it's exactly what I did to grow my network and develop my profile. Offer a free 30-minute seminar straight after networking events on your area of expertise:

✔ Is your thing presentation skills? Run a 30-minute session on using your body language to project confidence.

✔ You understand how to get Microsoft Excel to do stuff? Tell people to bring their laptops for a 30-minute master class on five top tips that can save them time.

✔ Are you a coach? Set up a 'magnificent mindset' workshop detailing how your attitude can influence your success at networking events.

✔ Are you a builder or tradesperson? Run a seminar on ten things everyone should do this season to safeguard their property and prevent damage.

I could go on, but you get the point. Get to know the people in your networking group and then arrange to have the meeting room for an extra 30 minutes next week. And don't just deliver your mini-seminar once; repeat it, offer it to different groups and let everyone see that not only do you know your stuff but you're also prepared to put some of your expertise out there.

The result – some people use the knowledge and tell everyone what a great person you are. Others listen and realise they need an expert to do it for them. The first expert they think of will probably be you.

Use Social Media

Unfortunately, most people are still using social media to broadcast rather than listen.

Check out who else is talking about your town. Go to `search.twitter.com` and have a look. If someone has mentioned your town, look at their profile. If they own or run a business, follow them, engage with them, get to know them.

Don't try it just once and then tell me it doesn't work. Keep doing it. Some people will ignore you. Some won't like being contacted by a stranger. Others will engage with you and become part of your circle and you theirs.

Make it Easy for People to Buy from You

Make sure that your offering is packaged properly for your audience and that your audience understands the benefit to them of doing business with you. Even if you do have different packages for different audiences ensure that your potential customers find the value of your product easy to understand.

Then make it easy for people to contact and do business with you. Be everywhere. Network on Twitter, LinkedIn and Google+. Respond to messages and requests quickly and efficiently. If someone asks about your service, get straight on the phone and talk to them about it. If someone passes you a referral, deal with it now and get back the referrer to tell them you've done so.

Develop a reputation for being easy to deal with. If you also have a fantastic product, you'll be laughing.

Understand that Networking is Working

Just by considering how to make networking more productive for you, you're getting value out of networking. Use your networking experience as a constant journey to refine and improve your offering, your service, your product, your communication skills, your social media footprint, your network of contacts, your presentations skills and your suppliers.

Enter every networking environment determined to discover something from each person you meet. It doesn't matter what. Even if you realise that you don't want to deal with them and they don't want to deal with you, you've saved yourself lots of time in the future!

Networking is always working and your business will always benefit.

Chapter 21

Ten Networking Gaffes to Avoid

I hope that, with this book in your hands, you're starting to get networking right.

But even if you only read this chapter, you can at least make sure you're getting it less wrong!

Talking Only About Yourself

This is the biggest mistake I witness on my networking travels. In no other sales environment would it be sensible to talk only about yourself, what you do, how brilliant your products are and why people should buy from you.

In any other sales environment you'd ask a little about the other person, establish some commonality and then find out about their needs and requirements before establishing whether your product or service might help.

Do you want to end a conversation with the other person thinking, 'What an interesting guy; and he was really interested in me. When he follows up I really must make sure I find out some more about what he does' or the alternative, 'Goodness, that man couldn't stop talking about himself; I'll make sure I avoid him in future'?

I've seen people miss huge opportunities by only talking about themselves, as well as someone offending me and another attendee by not asking before he tried to sell us stuff.

A wise person once said: 'You have one mouth and two ears. Use them in that proportion.'

Overrunning

If the introduction is supposed to be 40 seconds, stick to 40 seconds. If it's 60 seconds, stick to 60 seconds.

If anything, less is more in your introduction. You'll be struggling to maintain people's attention anyway as they think about their breakfast and mentally rehearse their own introduction. Keep your introduction short, memorable and to the point.

If everyone else in the room has stuck to the timings but you decide to overshoot, what does that say about you? That you think your message is much more important than theirs, that's what. Follow protocol and avoid getting a bad reputation.

Being Late

If you're going to a business networking meeting for the first time, check and double-check when it starts. You do *not* want to be the person who rolls in half-way through proceedings and you don't want to miss your opportunity to present yourself.

Arrive when you're meant to and allow yourself half an hour at the end of the meeting so you don't have to rush off and miss any important introductions.

Whispering during Other People's Introductions

You may have just realised that you *really* want a one-to-one with the person who's just spoken. You may have a vital piece of information that you want to pass onto someone else.

But what's important to the person on their feet is being able to speak without being distracted. No matter how important your piece of news, whispering to others while someone else is introducing themselves just comes across as rude.

Write down whatever you need to remember to say, and deal with it when the introductions are over. Don't risk offending someone else.

Ridiculing or Disrespecting Your Competitors

I had a one-to-one with someone recently. He asked me if I was using a particular service and I explained that I was buying it from another company. He then proceeded to ridicule that company, questioning their ethics and stating that I was making a mistake by using them.

Maybe I should've told him earlier on in the conversation that I was buying the service from a member of my own family!

Never disrespect the competition. Play to your own strengths; identify your unique selling points and how to market them.

Adding People to Your Mailing List without Permission

'Hi STEFAN THOMAS, we met at a networking meeting and I thought I would send you our latest 2,000-word email bringing you up-to-date with our latest services and news.'

We didn't 'meet'. We were in the same room and someone asked me for a business card and proceeded to add me, without my permission, to their mailing list.

Adding someone to your mailing list without their permission is likely to put their back up. Everyone's dealing with far too many emails as a matter of course and, on top of that, you run the risk of being labelled a spammer.

If you want to add people to your mailing list, ask them first and respect their decision. You'll make many more friends and people are much more likely to read your missives if they agreed to be added in the first place.

Judging a Book by Its Cover

Never underestimate anyone else in the room. You really never know who you're talking to, who they could be connected to or what they might go on to become in the future.

Networking is about building and growing relationships. You never know where a relationship may go, so don't judge it before it's even started. I've seen hundreds of connections made between the most seemingly unlikely contacts.

Keep an open mind. Talk to everyone.

Not Following Up

If you say you're going to call someone, do so. If you convince me that I need your service but you forget to follow up, I may forget why I needed it in the first place. Worse, I may remember why I needed it when I meet someone else who provides the same service and who *does* remember to follow up.

Make notes. Make the calls you promised to make. Keep in touch with your contacts in-between real-life meetings. Make it easier, not harder, for people to buy from you.

Treating Networking as a One-Off Sale

You're very unlikely to sell something at your first networking meeting. People at networking events get very used to people who just drop in when they have something to sell and drop out again when they don't. The trick with networking is to build your network while you don't need it so that it's there when you do.

Keep networking as a constant and regular activity, rather than just appearing when you need to hit an end of quarter target. Desperation doesn't sell.

Forgetting to Smile

I'm amazed by the number of people who arrive at networking events looking as though they're carrying the world's problems on their shoulders. I remember meeting someone new at a networking event who started his conversation by telling me about his awful journey, that business was terrible at the moment, that he was surprised more attendees hadn't shown up and he didn't like anything on the menu . . . and at that point my mind drifted off to a happier place.

If you're having a terrible day/week/month/hair day, use the energy of the others in the room to lift you. Don't use your energy to bring everyone else down.

People like to be around people who lift them. If you can be that person, you attract people to you at networking events. If you decide to be miserable you turn people away and may make the misguided decision that networking isn't for you.

Index

Notes

About the Author

Stefan Thomas first walked into a business networking meeting in late November 2005, following an 18-year career in estate agency.

Being terrified by the experience at first, Stef came to realise that there might be something in this networking lark and persevered, firstly with independent local groups and then BNI; before reading two lines in the local paper about something called 4Networking which had launched that morning. He registered on their website, got a call from the MD and, less than a week later, walked into his first 4N meeting.

Stef attended as many meetings as possible, learning his craft along the way. He started getting a reputation both within 4N and in other business spheres as someone who knew how to network and could teach others too.

Shortly afterwards Stef was hired by a national retail group to apply his networking expertise to their shop floor staff, giving them the skills and confidence to approach and engage customers in easy conversation.

Now a regular speaker on networking at business shows and other events, Stef is recognised as an expert on networking.

Stef became a Director of 4Networking Ltd in 2012, a position of which he's immensely proud.

Stef lives in Oxfordshire and has three sons. If you follow him on social media you'll know that he still spends too much time in the mosh pit at various rock gigs up and down the UK – something he's been doing since 1984.

You can contact Stef on Twitter @NoRedBraces; on LinkedIn at uk.linkedin.com/in/noredbraces/; on Facebook at facebook.com/noredbraces, and on Google+ https://plus.google.com/+StefanThomas.

Dedication

Business Networking For Dummies is dedicated to Joseph, George and Patrick. The three people who remind me, every day, what all of this is for.

Author's Acknowledgements

There are a ton of people I need to thank for their support in the creation of this book. If I managed to miss you out of this list, that in no way diminishes my huge gratitude.

Firstly, from Wiley, the publishers of the *For Dummies* series of books, thanks to Claire Ruston for having the faith in my abilities to commission me to write this book, Rachael Chilvers for keeping me on track and guiding me during the writing process and Raichelle Weller for so expertly handling the marketing.

Thank you to my co-directors in 4Networking, Brad Burton (Managing Director) and Terry Cooper (Chairman) for helping me to be in the right place at the right time. That's what we do. Their patience with me and occasional kick up the backside when I needed it played a much bigger part than they will ever know.

Thank you to the various business networks and other business organisations out there who helped me with research about their setups. Specifically for taking the time to talk to me: Charlie Lawson of BNI, Dave Clarke of NRG, Alex Butler of KindredHQ, Jan Pearce of The Great British Business Show, Emma Wilkins of The Welsh Business Show, Warren Cass of Business Scene and Mark Linton of The Business Growth Show.

Finally, thank you to the many thousands of people I've met during my networking journey. Each one of you has contributed to this.

Publisher's Acknowledgements

Project Editor: Rachael Chilvers

Commissioning Editor: Claire Ruston

Associate Commissioning Editor:
Ben Kemble

Development Editor: Kelly Ewing

Copyeditor: Kim Vernon

Proofreader: Kate O'Leary

Technical Editor: Ben Kench, The
Business Booster Ltd

Publisher: Miles Kendall

Cover Photos: © iStockphoto.com/
rafal_olechowski

Project Coordinator: Sheree Montgomery

Take Dummies with you everywhere you go!

Whether you're excited about e-books, want more from the web, must have your mobile apps, or swept up in social media, Dummies makes everything easier.

Visit Us	Like Us	Follow Us	Watch Us
Join Us	**Pin Us**	**Circle Us**	**Shop Us**

FOR DUMMIES

A Wiley Brand

BUSINESS

Small Business Marketing For Dummies
978-1-118-73077-5

Pop Up Business For Dummies
978-1-118-44349-1

Starting & Running a Business All-in-One For Dummies
978-1-119-97527-4

MUSIC

Mandolin For Dummies
978-1-119-94276-4

Ukulele For Dummies
978-0-470-97799-6

Piano For Dummies
978-0-470-49644-2

DIGITAL PHOTOGRAPHY

Digital Photography For Dummies
978-1-118-09203-3

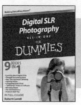

Digital SLR Photography All-in-One For Dummies
978-0-470-76878-5

Nikon D3100 For Dummies
978-1-118-00472-2

Algebra I For Dummies
978-0-470-55964-2

Anatomy & Physiology
For Dummies, 2nd Edition
978-0-470-92326-9

Asperger's Syndrome For Dummies
978-0-470-66087-4

Basic Maths For Dummies
978-1-119-97452-9

Body Language For Dummies,
2nd Edition
978-1-119-95351-7

Bookkeeping For Dummies,
3rd Edition
978-1-118-34689-1

British Sign Language For Dummies
978-0-470-69477-0

Cricket for Dummies, 2nd Edition
978-1-118-48032-8

Currency Trading For Dummies,
2nd Edition
978-1-118-01851-4

Cycling For Dummies
978-1-118-36435-2

Diabetes For Dummies, 3rd Edition
978-0-470-97711-8

eBay For Dummies, 3rd Edition
978-1-119-94122-4

Electronics For Dummies
All-in-One For Dummies
978-1-118-58973-1

English Grammar For Dummies
978-0-470-05752-0

French For Dummies, 2nd Edition
978-1-118-00464-7

Guitar For Dummies, 3rd Edition
978-1-118-11554-1

IBS For Dummies
978-0-470-51737-6

Keeping Chickens For Dummies
978-1-119-99417-6

Knitting For Dummies, 3rd Edition
978-1-118-66151-2

FOR DUMMIES

A Wiley Brand

SELF-HELP

978-0-470-66541-1

978-1-119-99264-6

978-0-470-66086-7

LANGUAGES

978-0-470-68815-1

978-1-119-97959-3

978-0-470-69477-0

HISTORY

978-0-470-68792-5

978-0-470-74783-4

978-0-470-97819-1

Laptops For Dummies 5th Edition
978-1-118-11533-6

Management For Dummies, 2nd Edition
978-0-470-97769-9

Nutrition For Dummies, 2nd Edition
978-0-470-97276-2

Office 2013 For Dummies
978-1-118-49715-9

Organic Gardening For Dummies
978-1-119-97706-3

Origami Kit For Dummies
978-0-470-75857-1

Overcoming Depression For Dummies
978-0-470-69430-5

Physics I For Dummies
978-0-470-90324-7

Project Management For Dummies
978-0-470-71119-4

Psychology Statistics For Dummies
978-1-119-95287-9

Renting Out Your Property For Dummies, 3rd Edition
978-1-119-97640-0

Rugby Union For Dummies, 3rd Edition
978-1-119-99092-5

Stargazing For Dummies
978-1-118-41156-8

Teaching English as a Foreign Language For Dummies
978-0-470-74576-2

Time Management For Dummies
978-0-470-77765-7

Training Your Brain For Dummies
978-0-470-97449-0

Voice and Speaking Skills For Dummies
978-1-119-94512-3

Wedding Planning For Dummies
978-1-118-69951-5

WordPress For Dummies, 5th Edition
978-1-118-38318-6

Think you can't learn it in a day? Think again!

The *In a Day* e-book series from *For Dummies* gives you quick and easy access to learn a new skill, brush up on a hobby, or enhance your personal or professional life — all in a day. Easy!